MOTHER CH'

MOTHER CHURCH

Ecclesiology and Ecumenism

CARL E. BRAATEN

FORTRESS PRESS
MINNEAPOLIS

MOTHER CHURCH
Ecclesiology and Ecumenism

The author wishes gratefully to acknowledge the kindness of several journals in which earlier versions of these chapters appeared, including *Journal of Ecumenical Studies, Lutheran Forum, Ex Auditu,* and *Interpretation.*

Cover design: Mike Mihelich
Cover graphic: Design taken from Augsburg Fortress parament (silk embroidery on silk). Pomegranites symbolize fertility and growth.
Interior book design: The HK Scriptorium, Inc.

Library of Congress Cataloging in Publication Data

Braaten, Carl E., 1929–
    Mother church : ecclesiology and ecumenism / Carl E. Braaten.
        p.   cm.
    Includes bibliographical references.
    ISBN 0-8006-3082-3 (alk. paper)
    1. Church. 2. Church—Teaching office. 3. Christian union.
  4. Ecumenical movement. 5. Christian union—Lutheran Church.
  6. Christian union—Catholic Church. 7. Lutheran Church—Doctrines.
  8. Catholic Church—Doctrines. I. Title.
BV600.2.B66 1998
262—dc21   98-11785
                                            CIP

Manufactured in the U.S.A.   AF 1-3082
02 01 00 99 98 1   2   3   4   5   6   7   8   9   10

To my grandchildren

Jennifer

James

Sylvia

Linnea

Sean

Jake

Dana

Sonja

Ransom

You cannot have God for your father unless you have the church for your mother.

—St. Cyprian

I embrace the church, the communion of saints, as my holy mother, and in a conscious act of faith I make my own all the spiritual blessings that the church represents.

—Martin Luther

Contents

The Century of the Church

THE SEARCH FOR a truly ecumenical doctrine of the church is one of the most creative developments of twentieth-century theology. In the 1920s Bishop Otto Dibelius wrote a book that carried the title *Das Jahrhundert der Kirche* (The Century of the Church), a prophetic signal of things to come. Within a decade he was embroiled in the German "church struggle" (*Kirchenkampf*). In 1933 he was removed from pastoral office by the National Socialists and then became a leader in the resistance movement of the Confessing Church. When Germany was partitioned after World War II, Bishop Dibelius fought for the integrity and independence of the church against the totalitarian state under Communist rule as he had done against the Nazis. At the forefront of the ecumenical movement, Dibelius was fittingly elected president of the World Council of Churches in 1954 (Evanston). His ministry was a living symbol of the very churchliness—of thought and action, of theology and service—that he called for in his book on the twentieth century as the age in which the church was coming into its own.

In support of Bishop Dibelius's thesis I would call attention to Karl Barth's monumental achievement, his *Church Dogmatics*. The work is all the more spectacular in that he probed the truth of dogmatics for the one church in spite of the divisions and differences between Orthodox, Roman Catholic, and Protestant Christians. On another front, the German Catholic theologian, Romano Guardini, wrote after World War I: "An event of incalculable importance has begun: the church is awakening in people's souls."[1] In quoting this statement

Cardinal Joseph Ratzinger elaborated: "The Second Vatican Council was the fruit of this awakening."[2]

The title of this book is *Mother Church*. Its chapters tell the story of my own growing awareness of the place of the church in the divine scheme of things. I write in the conviction that Protestants, Lutherans among them, need to rediscover the idea and experience of the church as mother, which characterized the fathers of the ancient church. In Tertullian, Cyprian, Origen, Augustine, and many others, we find a multiplicity of renderings of the famous saying: "You cannot have God for your father unless you have the church for your mother."[3] For the ancient fathers the notion of the church as mother was more than a beautiful phrase and lovely metaphor. It signifies life as we are born from her womb; it signifies identity as we are offspring of the bride of Christ; it signifies nourishment as from her hands we receive food and drink, the very body and blood of our Lord Jesus Christ.

Not only the ancient fathers but also the Reformers, Martin Luther and John Calvin, used the image of "mother church" in continuity with the great tradition. In his *Large Catechism,* Luther wrote that the Holy Spirit "has a unique community in the world. It is the mother that begets and bears every Christian through the Word of God."[4] Calvin astonished some of his followers by seeming to sound too Catholic when he wrote in his *Institutes of the Christian Religion:*

> But as our present design is to treat of the visible Church, we may learn even from the title mother, how useful and even necessary it is for us to know her; since there is no other way of entrance into life, unless we are conceived by her, born of her, nourished at her breast, and continually preserved under her care and government till we are divested of this mortal flesh, and "become like the angels." For our infirmity will not admit of our dismission from her school; we must continue under her instruction and discipline to the end of our lives. It is also to be remarked, that out of her bosom there can be no hope of remission of sins, or any salvation.[5]

Philip du Plessis-Mornay, one of Calvin's loyal disciples, later wrote on the first page of his *Treatise on the Church*: "God has willed that the church should be honored and recognized as Mother by all those whose

Father he has designed to be."[6] Both Luther and Calvin had learned such filial piety toward the church from their master teacher, Augustine, who wrote: "Behold the womb of Mother Church: see how she groans and is in travail to bring you forth and guide you on into the light of faith."[7]

Something happened to this belief in mother church on the way to modern Protestantism. Few statements have been more telling than Friedrich Schleiermacher's dogmatic proposition describing the antithesis of Protestantism and Catholicism: "The former [i.e., Protestantism] makes the individual's relation to the church dependent on his relation to Christ, while the latter [i.e., Catholicism] makes the individual's relation to Christ dependent on his relation to the church."[8] The antithesis became sharp in many varieties of Protestantism, liberal, revivalist, sectarian, and conservative. Stress was placed on the religious personality, on the subjective experiences and feelings of the individual soul. Not much room was left for the church, neither for its creeds and confessions nor for its liturgical life and church offices.

The interpretation of Luther in German Protestantism, in the line from Schleiermacher through Albrecht Ritschl to Adolf von Harnack, placed Luther unambiguously on the Protestant side of the great divide. On the relation between Christ and the church, Luther's theology was reconstructed in the image of the Protestant experience. The German reformer was championed as the leader of faith and freedom. The Catholic elements in Luther's writings were dismissed as pieces of eggshell sticking to the newborn chick in the process of being hatched. Supposedly Luther's inner life of faith and the external trappings of church tradition that overlay it could be sorted out only later by his Protestant interpreters.

The first chapter of this book reflects the earliest phase of my ecumenical experience as a theologian. Pope John XXIII had convoked the Second Vatican Council, and I was invited to give an ecumenical address to a group of Lutheran pastors in Illinois. The subject I chose was "The Tragedy of the Reformation and the Return to Catholicity." That marked the beginning of my quest for an ecumenically valid ecclesiology. The basic model that guided my proposals for the ecumenical movement at that time was the image of Protestants in exile.

The suggestion came from an article by George Lindbeck entitled, "A Protestant View of the Ecclesiology of the Roman Catholic Church," in which the exile metaphor characterized the situation of Protestantism. Lindbeck wrote:

> The Catholic Church was for the early Protestants the one and only church, it was their home church, it was their ecclesiastical homeland—but it was under enemy occupation. The government had become tyrannical. It drove out not only those who would reform it, but even those who asked for nothing more than the freedom to preach the gospel. There was nothing to do except to form a government, an ecclesiastical order, in exile. But the Reformers at first no more thought of this as a new, a second church than de Gaulle thought of his war-time regime as a replacement, a substitute for France.[9]

This image of being in exile continues to remind me of the provisional character of Lutheranism and of the necessity of the ecumenical movement to work for the reunion of separated Christians and ecclesial communities in the one, holy, catholic, and apostolic church.

The mood is not running high in favor of continuing the ecumenical dialogues spawned by the Second Vatican Council. Disenchantment has set in prematurely; the goal of unity has not yet been reached. The churches are still badly divided. Meanwhile a possibly more serious problem has arisen. The churches are inwardly permeated by the weakening of distinctively Christian beliefs, by a willingness to accommodate various impulses of the *Zeitgeist*, and by a combination of biblical illiteracy among the laity and biblical infidelity among the clergy, theologians, and church leaders. The high toleration of heresy and apostasy causes heart failure in the Christian organism. The most recent chapters written for this book focus on the crisis of authority in the churches that lies at the root of the current ecumenical malaise. Uniting churches that have lost their way would be like the blind leading the blind. Why should church leaders jet around the world dealing with the extramural affairs of their communities when the fires of controversy back home are destroying the faith and confidence of their people?

I believe, however, that the ecumenical movement and its aim of church unity are too important to put on a back burner. The struggles for gospel fidelity within the churches and for full communion between the churches belong together because both arise out of the one apostolic faith. To that end I am devoting this book. True ecumenism is rooted in the doctrines of the gospel and in the life of worshiping communities. There is an ecumenism born of the flesh of ecclesiastical politics that shaves the truth for the sake of harmony, and there is an ecumenism born of the Spirit that unites people at the grassroots in faith, hope, and love. The ecumenical assets of the World Council of Churches are put in jeopardy when its leaders seem to have surrendered the search for unity based on faith and doctrine in exchange for a social and political agenda dictated by the world.

The future of the ecumenical movement cannot be separated from the future of the one holy catholic church of Christ on earth. The hope and the promise of unity can be encouraged by the "ecclesiology of communion" that has captured the imagination of theologians across the ecumenical spectrum—Orthodox, Roman Catholic, Anglican, Lutheran, Reformed, and others. The vision of the church as a communion of churches informs and inspires the work in which I am presently engaged. About six years ago I left classroom teaching at the Lutheran School of Theology at Chicago to found and direct the Center for Catholic and Evangelical Theology, located in Northfield, Minnesota. This Center has become the focal point of a theological movement from across denominations and disciplines that reflects an awakening of the church on American soil.

Doing theology *pro ecclesia* has been largely replaced by the religious studies approach in the American academy. That approach also enters the theological seminaries of the church when teachers who, knowing no better way, simply pass on the methods and results they learned in their doctoral programs. The academy and not the church provides the context and criteria for religious reflection, and Christianity is treated like any other religion.

The project of liberal theology has always been to search for some elusive and illusory essence of Christianity—some particular modification of the more general essence of religion. But Christianity, like religion, is an abstraction; it does not exist, and it certainly did not exist in New Testament times. What we have rather are churches, concrete communities, whose living traditions, beginning with the canonical Scriptures, provide the primary data for theological reflection. We believe that specifically *Christian* theology is possible only within the context of the church, the *koinonia* or fellowship of believers with Christ and with one another as members of his body, faithful to the apostolic foundations, and obedient to the catholic norms of mother church.

This book is an example of theology that some will label as "evangelical catholic." I will not complain about this; I have been using the term for a long time to characterize my self-understanding as a Lutheran theologian. I believe Luther was an evangelical catholic. The Lutheran movement named after him—against his will—is truest to Luther's reforming intent when it understands that catholic and evangelical are complementary concepts. They possess their truth in constant orientation toward each other. By becoming more evangelical, the church will be more catholic; and by becoming more catholic, she will be more evangelical. People who say that evangelical catholic is an oxymoron simply fail to understand what the Reformation was all about.

In Reformation theology the church has been defined as the creature of the word (*creatura verbi divini*) or of the gospel (Luther: "*Ecclesia enim creatura est evangelii*"). I come from a Lutheran tradition that has always approached ecclesiology through Christology. This approach, however, is not uniquely Lutheran. Yves Congar, a French Catholic theologian, used the term *Christomonism* to characterize and criticize the prevailing view of the church in Catholic theology prior to Vatican II. Thanks to the influence of Eastern Orthodox theologians, our attention has been increasingly directed to the patristic tradition. There we find a trinitarian perspective on ecclesiology, one in which the doctrine of the Spirit is coequal with the Word. The church is the work of the Holy Trinity, and the Trinity is the source (Father), image (Son), and goal (Spirit) of the church. The Trinity is the foundational principle of a theology *pro ecclesia*.

The theological imbalance that results from one-sidedly deriving the church from Christology is paralleled by an equally one-sided emphasis on the Word at the expense of the Sacraments in post-Reformation Protestantism. The primary task is the proclamation of the word of God. True! But typically for Protestants this tends to be restricted to audible words of preaching. But what happens when the preaching goes sour, which unfortunately is not a rare occurrence. Then what? The preached word is a sacrament that calls people to salvation through judgment and grace. This is one channel, and it often gets clogged with the scum of human opinions—politically correct editorializing. Another channel alongside is the visible words of bread and wine, the Holy Sacrament of Christ's body and blood.

The Eucharist Makes the Church. So reads the title of a recent book by Paul McPartlan, in which the author expounds and compares the theologies of Henri de Lubac, a French Catholic, and John Zizioulas, a Greek Orthodox.[10] Without renouncing the Reformation heritage that strives for faithful preaching of the word, we are intent on rectifying the imbalance that plagues Protestantism—insensitivity to the sacrament of the real presence of Christ, his body and blood, in, with, and under the bread we break and the wine we drink. Again, it is the Orthodox who may help Protestants to recover a eucharistic theology and practice that lead to a high doctrine of the church. We can appropriate the truth of Pope John Paul II's saying that, separated from the Orthodox church, the Catholic church is breathing with only one lung. It is our hope that Protestants too might learn to breathe with two lungs—both Word and Sacrament. What defines the church is the living presence incarnate in the Eucharist, where Christ and his community are bodily one. The church is Christ as his bodily presence in the world, prefiguring the future of the world in the kingdom of God.

For Luther, the church was essentially the "communion of saints," the assembly of those who gather in fellowship with Christ and with one another and partake of the holy gifts of God freely given to his chosen people. However, new and deeper levels of meaning of the biblical idea of *koinonia* are being explored in light of the trinitarian foundation of the church. These new understandings of *koinonia* have fascinating implications for the ecumenical aim of reuniting the divided churches. The church is a communion structured in the image and likeness of the trinitarian communion of persons. In his book *Being as Communion,* Zizioulas has brilliantly spelled out the ontological dimensions of a "communion-ecclesiology." He writes:

The mystery of the church, even in its institutional dimensions, is deeply bound to the being of man, to the being of the world and to the very being of God. In virtue of this bond, so characteristic of patristic thought, ecclesiology assumes a marked importance, not only for all aspects of theology, but also for the existential needs of man in every age.[11]

Communion-ecclesiology lays stress on the ontological priority of the local church because the church of God is always concretely actualized "where the Word is preached and the Sacraments are administered." Here we have a point of contact between Lutheran and Orthodox ecclesiology, but it remains underdeveloped. The ecumenical issue of great importance is that of the relationship between the local eucharistic assemblies and the regional and universal manifestations of the one holy catholic church. Local congregations exist in eucharistic fellowship with each other, and that level of communion also participates in ecclesial reality. The universal church is a communion of communions, a "church of churches."[12] There are ministries and signs of unity at each level of ecclesial communion—presbyters (pastors or priests), bishops, and pope. There remain theological disputes concerning all of them that stand as obstacles in the way of church unity.

What prospects does a trinitarian-based communion-ecclesiology offer to the ecumenical quest for unity? The path to unity is impeded by sin that lies at the heart of every historic division in church history. But sin can be forgiven and blotted out. Unity is a gift that only God can grant at a time of his own choosing but not without our participation. The ecclesiology of communion opens up the greatest possibilities for reciprocal acceptance among the churches. The alternatives are to give up on the ecumenical movement, to nullify the convergence and consensus reached in the dialogues, to sink back into disillusionment, or to stoke the fires of the old interchurch rivalries between Catholics, Protestants, and Orthodox.

Ecumenism exists not only on the institutional hierarchical level where official dialogues take place between leaders of communities and agreements are theologically and politically negotiated for reconciliation and communion. Ecumenism exists, equally importantly, at the spiritual level where the Spirit of God is at work in the hearts and minds of the people of God across ecclesiastical boundary lines. Both are necessary. The institutional level should be a sign and servant of what the Spirit of God is doing to build up the one body of which Christ is the head. Otherwise the organized institutional church can become a dying and empty shell, what Harnack called "the aroma of an empty bottle" and worse, possibly an enemy of the kingdom of God in league with the anti-Christ. Sometimes the two levels come close to being the inside and the outside of the one holy catholic and apostolic church. At other times, however, they fight against each other. When the ecclesiastical powers-that-be persecute the faithful, then confessing movements of reform and resistance break out here and there, rallying the faithful under the cross of suffering and martyrdom as witnesses of the coming kingdom. The four horsemen of the Apocalypse ride the earth slaughtering the souls of the faithful for the testimonies they offer to the word of God.

What if we all patch things up ecumenically at the highest institutional level, while internally all our church bodies are being eaten away by viruses that invade from the surrounding "culture of death"? What if on the threshold of full communion between our churches we look inward to find that each of them is eviscerated by heresies and is on the brink of schism? What if we can no longer be sure that we in the same denomination hold the same faith, worship the same God, baptize into the same name, and proclaim the same gospel? What if we are no longer in fellowship with members of our own church? Such a scenario appears to many observers dangerously close to the way things are heading in many of our church bodies. A life and death struggle for the confessional center is going on in all Protestant denominations. The confessional center is not the concoction of conservatives but simply the evangelical catholic faith in continuity with the Scriptures and the apostolic tradition.

Ecumenism is alive at the spiritual level. A realignment is taking place without anyone in particular orchestrating it. New dividing issues have cropped up. New lines between heresy and orthodoxy may need to be drawn. The ecumenical dialogues have not done that. In general they have not treated the new issues that have seized denominations by the throat. Meanwhile, our church bodies lack structures of authority that can deal with the crisis of faith and doctrine. Even some bishops take the law into their own hands and often are not subject to discipline within their churches. Some of the chapters in this book focus on the problem of teaching authority in the church. This seems to me to be the chief common problem in virtually all the ecumenical dialogues.

Ecclesiology and ecumenism were the focal point of my theological writing in the 1960s and early 1970s and now again in the 1990s. A few critics have remarked how my mind has changed over the decades, given my current efforts on behalf of an evangelical and catholic turn in theology. There are things I am certain that I would no longer say or would not say in the same way. Thirty years of dialogical ecumenical experience count for something. And my perception of the situation in church and theology has changed. I believe we are now in a struggle for the soul of the church, for faithfulness to the Scriptures, and for continuity with the creedal and confessional traditions of the church. The roots of my commitment to an evangelical and catholic perspective in theology, however, are readily discernible in the earliest chapters of this book.

CHAPTER ONE

The Tragedy of the Reformation and the Return to Catholicity

LET US BEGIN WITH A PARABLE taken from a slice of the history of World War II.[1] In June of 1940 Adolf Hitler's army invaded and conquered France. Marshal Pétain became the head of state under Hitler and formulated what was notoriously known as the Vichy Government. Pétain acted as the puppet of Hitler's occupation army. Many a loyal and patriotic Frenchman, however, for the love of the true fatherland protested against the Vichy government. A man came forth—a kind of savior figure for France at the crucial hour. He was General Charles de Gaulle. De Gaulle raised the cross of Lorraine in Britain and became the rallying point for all free Frenchmen who joined with him in the fight to liberate their beloved country. Frenchmen became divided. Some were loyal to the Vichy government of Pétain, and others joined the Free French forces in exile. Their purpose in being outside of France was to preserve the glory of France, to protest against a false government, to struggle for the liberation of their homeland, and on V-Day to be reunited with their fellow countrymen.

What if those free Frenchmen forgot the reason for their exile, became accustomed to life outside of France, lost interest in returning, and began to think and act as if what was meant to be a temporary arrangement and provisional expedient in an emergency situation had actually become for them a permanent home and satisfying establishment? Suppose they ignored the cause of liberation for which they rallied around de Gaulle and instead set up a new government in some other colony, calling it France, enjoying their newfound life so much that the very thought of ever going back to the land of their birth made them ill. Now, if that would have happened, one would call it a tragedy—a tragedy very much like the tragedy of the Reformation.

The Tragedy of the Reformation

The Reformation witnessed the split in the Western church. Christians became divided. The Reformers made their protest against Rome on behalf of the whole church, out of love and loyalty to the truly catholic church. After the split came, they continued to work for the reform of the church, the renewal of Christian life, and the reunion of the alienated parties. The furthest thing from Martin Luther's mind was to make his reform movement into an independent church bearing his name and that would exist permanently outside of and in competition with the Roman Catholic Church.

The tragedy is great enough that the split was necessary, as we believe, for the sake of the truth of the gospel. A still greater tragedy is that what was intended to be only a temporary situation, an interim period, entirely for the sake of reforming the one church, has become a permanent arrangement with no end in sight. The Reformation was not intended to bring about a Protestant Church, much less a collection of Protestant churches. The Reformation was a movement of protest for the sake of the one church. The Reformation was a necessity, but we Protestants have made a virtue out of a necessity thereby deluding ourselves.

We cannot deny that Protestantism has turned out quite differently from anything Luther and the other Reformers had in mind. The Reformation was intended as a call to catholicity and away from the Romanization of the Western church. Instead, the Reformation produced a conglomeration of Protestant communities, none of which has really dared to call itself catholic. Søren Kierkegaard often bemoaned the fact that Lutheranism, which started out to be a corrective movement within the Roman Catholic Church, has become a fixed condition that is in sore need of correction.

We are beginning to see more clearly today the essence of the tragedy of the Reformation. To be sure, it was tragedy enough that the late medieval church fell into such an abysmal state of degeneration; it was also a tragedy that Rome refused to listen to Luther's call to reform and drove him into exile. It was, therefore, also a tragedy that during the interim period of separation from Rome the Reformers had to create and set in motion the ecclesiastical machinery necessary for the functioning of a church, its preaching, teaching, and pastoral work. The greatest tragedy of all is that the heirs of the Reformation for generations to follow got used to the separation, took it for a permanent condition, and gave less and less thought to reconciliation with the Roman Catholic Church.

Jaroslav Pelikan devoted a chapter in his book *The Riddle of Roman Catholicism* to the "tragic necessity of the reformation." It was as tragic as it was necessary. A chief cause of bad relations and the chief obstacle to better relations between Protestants and Catholics is the lack of insight into the causes, conditions, and consequences of the sixteenth-century crisis and schism in the church. Roman Catholics have agreed that the Reformation was tragic, but few have seen its necessity.[2] Protestants have agreed that the Reformation was necessary, but few have felt with deep and lasting pain its tragedy. Protestants have forgotten their reason for existence as Protestants, as *protesters* against a false government and against a tyrannical regime in their own homeland. It is as if anti-Castro Cubans, who left or were driven out of Cuba, lost their zeal to go back, got good jobs and settled down for good in New York or Miami, and, so taken up with their own parochial pursuits and personal pleasures, abandoned any sense of concern or responsibility for what happens in Cuba.

One of the soundest reasons for expecting the riplets of reconciliation on the troubled waters of our church relations to pile up into a tidal wave driving relentlessly toward the shores of reunion, is the new in-depth understanding of Luther and the Reformation that in the last decades has occurred on both sides. Protestants now see that the Reformation was a necessary tragedy, and Catholics see that it was a tragic necessity. There is good and evil on both sides. As Pope John XXIII said so succinctly, "Responsibility is divided," and so, hopefully, "let us come together, let us make an end of our divisions."[3]

The New Catholic View of Luther

A massive amount of research, with startling results, has been conducted by Roman Catholic scholars on Luther and the Reformation. Let us take only a sample here and there of some of the newer elements in the Roman Catholic view of the Reformation. Perhaps the most important clue behind it all is the acceptance and application of the historical method right across-the-board. First, the historical method was applied with useful results to the Bible itself. Catholic and Protestant scholars discovered they could work in closer cooperation, achieving remarkable consensus even on exegetical matters underlying traditional confessional controversies. Next, the historical method was applied to the Reformation period. Luther could now be interpreted in light of the conditions which produced him, and not only in light of the conditions which he produced. A truly historical perspective, not merely a polemical construction, has gradually come to predominate.

The Catholic picture of Luther at the beginning of this century was painted in lurid colors by Henri Denifle, the Dominican historian, and Hartmann Grisar, the Jesuit. Their huge tomes, with all the apparatus and appearances of scientific-historical research, painted Luther as a sensualist whose sexual passions produced the Reformation and whose pathological mind invented the spurious doctrine of justification by faith alone, and "whose mind was like a cesspool and with a mouth to match."[4]

Around 1940 a new picture of Luther began to emerge. Joseph Lortz began to publish his works on the Reformation. On the one side, he depicted in utter frankness the worldliness of the papacy, the abuses in church practice and superstitions of piety, and the decadence of late scholasticism. On the other side, he portrayed Luther in sympathetic terms as the religious monk posing the ultimate question of life, the question of salvation. Against the nominalistic theology and indulgence piety of late medievalism, Luther placed his theology of the cross—his absolute trust in God's grace, not in his own works; his reliance upon the Scriptures, not upon the opinions of the schoolmen; and his protest against superstition in low places and corruption in high places. In this context, Lortz said, the Roman Catholic Church today must definitely be on the side of Luther. He made other Roman Catholics see and accept the idea that Roman Catholics share in the guilt of schism.

Other Roman Catholic scholars have contributed equally to a recasting of the image of Luther. Johannes Hessen said that the message of the Reformation, anchored as it was in genuinely Roman Catholic history, must still be heard today. What ailed the church in Luther's day is still afflicting the church: intellectualism, moralism, sacramentalism, and institutionalism. Karl Adam called upon all those serious about the ecumenical dialogue to go back to Luther himself, for the starting point in the dialogue must be the dividing point. The gulf can be bridged between the confessions only after we retrace our steps and gain a real understanding from both sides on what went wrong. Yves Congar, the French Dominican, said that Luther must be seen as one in a long line of Reformers in the church. According to Congar, Luther addressed a question that the church at that time was in no position to answer, and which it still has never answered in a serious way. Certainly, he said, excommunication was no answer to the kind of legitimate questions Luther was asking. Certainly, the Council of Trent's response was not to Luther's basic intention and meaning but only to some of the extreme inferences that his disciples drew from his teachings. The Roman Catholic Church, with its purely anti-Protestant spirit since Trent, has not yet tried hard to understand Protestant concerns. Therefore, in closing her ears to her opponents and taking up a defensive posture, the church of Rome lost some of her own catholicity. Congar also hurled a challenge to the church today. The church today must be reformed in such a way that, had this reformed Catholic church existed in the sixteenth century, there would have been no need for such a violent explosion—a revolution.

Father Louis Bouyer, even more emphatically than any of the others, proposed the thesis that the positive principles of the Reformation were not an attack on Catholic faith and doctrine but were truly at home in the Catholic Church. Of course, Philip Melanchthon also affirmed that there is nothing in the Augsburg Confession that deviates from the Bible or the Catholic tradition, but to hear a Roman Catholic scholar state that Protestants are truly Catholic when they go deeply into the heart of the Reformation seems either like playing tricks with words or represents a radical shift in attitude. Protestants are not asked to give up the great slogans of the Reformation: grace alone, faith alone, Scripture alone, and Christ alone. They are only asked to understand them more deeply, and, when they do that, they are on their way to a rebirth of catholicity. Bouyer saw the Reformation as particularly tragic because, to the extent that the Protestants drew false and heretical inferences from those positive principles, the Catholics were driven to oppose the principles, and thereby, lost much of the good with the bad. Part of their own Catholic substance was sacrificed with the exclusion of the protesting Reformers from the Roman Catholic Church.

Evangelical Catholicity

Concurrent with this new understanding of Luther and the Reformation among Catholic scholars is a new self-criticism among Lutherans. It manifests itself as a desire to experience a new birth of catholicity—a recovery of catholic substance and principles that have been lost in Protestant history. It aims not merely to revitalize the Protestant communities for prolonged separate existence but to renew in them the longing to be integrated with their Roman brethren in the one catholic church. There is no doubt that a phenomenon we can best call *evangelical catholicity* is growing among Lutherans.

An evangelical catholic position holds, first of all, with K. E. Skydsgaard, leading Lutheran expert on Roman theology, that the church must at the same time be both "catholic" and "evangelical" because it must include both continuity and reformation. Catholic and evangelical are not opposite but "complementary concepts that only possess their truth in their constant orientation toward each other."[5] The will of the Reformation was precisely to become more evangelical by becoming truly more catholic. Historically, however, Lutherans have prided themselves for having vied with one another on having the truest, purest, and most unaltered, unadulterated evangelical doctrine. There has been, by contrast, a conspicuous silence and disinterest in regard to the meaning of confessing the catholicity of the church in the Apostles' and Nicene Creeds. Indifference to catholicity implies that it has become an empty word. The quest for the meaning of this word and for the experience of the reality it is meant to represent constitutes the chief business of today's ecumenical movement. Lutherans must be in the forefront of this quest, for they are among those who have lost much that is genuinely catholic.

Lutherans have been admirably zealous about posing the question, "What is the gospel?" They have held themselves to evangelical norms in their theology, but, with less zeal and certainly with less success, have they worried about where the true church is to be found and what visible historical form it should take. They have been much less concerned about the norm of catholicity in their theology. To say that the church is where the gospel is preached and where the sacraments are administered is true but not true enough because it says too little. It has nothing to say of relevance to the actual situation in the West where there are twenty sizable denominations preaching the gospel and administering the sacraments without manifesting precisely those marks of the church that we confess, namely, the unity and catholicity of the church.

We have lived in a strange paradoxical situation in which Protestants have been trying to have the gospel and its freedom without the church and its structure and Catholics have been trying to have a church with a superabundance of structure without the gospel. Of course, we are exaggerating for the sake of effect. On both sides it is a question of degrees. There are traces of churchly reality on the Protestant side, and there are living manifestations of genuine evangelical content and freedom on the Catholic side. The church must live within the polarity of order and freedom. Protestants have witnessed to the freedom but not to the order, thus leading to the anarchy, chaos, and libertarianism with which they are familiar. Catholics have witnessed to the order but not to the freedom, thus leading to the formalism and authoritarianism with which they are familiar. Both sides have had much to gain by meeting each other.

An evangelical catholic position has a high regard for the Reformation—appreciates its necessity—but sees its franchise as limited, provisional, and terminal, and always related to the Roman Catholic Church. It takes seriously the often glibly made statement: "Luther never intended to found a new church, but he was excommunicated." The thing to do when you're excommunicated, and you're convinced you're in the right, is to try to rectify those conditions which produced the wrong and finally to have the bans of excommunication withdrawn. Meanwhile, life must go on; the gospel must be preached, and people must be cared for. To those ends you set up a temporary government—a provisional ecclesiastical order—while in exile. You make the best out of a bad situation, but you don't make a virtue out of a necessity. That is what traditional Protestantism has done. Such Protestants are like exiles who lose the desire to rejoin their fellow countrymen but "become thoroughly acclimatized in their new ecclesiastical homes."[6] Many Protestants believe that it is enough to be against Rome to be Protestant, although they share none of Luther's reasons for his attack on the papacy. Lutherans who are evangelical catholics believe that each generation of Protestants must justify its continued separation from the Roman Catholic Church.

The End of the Protestant Era?

The inescapable question is then: Are we justified in continuing our separation? The Roman Catholic Church holds out an open invitation to return at any time. Many Protestants are so insecure in their independent existence that they feel insulted by the invitation. They feel psychologically threatened. They would rather be left alone. They tend to view the Reformation not as a movement for the sake of the Roman Catholic Church but as a new departure, the beginning of a new Christianity that leaps over the centuries back into the primitive church and Bible times. Evangelical Lutherans who make their protest for the sake of the catholicity of the church cannot do that. We must seriously ask today whether our continued separation is justified, and we must answer that question honestly, without rationalizing. That is, a church which claims to live by the justification of God alone (*sola gratia*) cannot honestly seek to justify itself. The justification for a continued separation must have theological and not psychological reasons. Hans Küng has written: "A protest, even though justified in its time, should not necessarily be repeated forever. Do Protestant preachers and theologians give enough thought to this?"[7]

Does the Reformation protest still need to be heard? That is one question that we must answer. Of course, the Reformation protest must always be heard in the church because that protest is not merely a negative thing bound to local conditions; it is also a positive message with application as universal as the sinful nature of humanity. The protest is the sounding forth of God's own protest, the judgment of law against human pride and self-assertiveness, and the justification by the gospel—God's acceptance of humans despite their sinfulness. The church stands or falls with the hearing of this message of law and gospel, judgment and salvation. The further question is: do we need a divided Christendom to preserve the preaching of that law and gospel in its truth, power, and purity? To use Paul Tillich's phrase in a different connection: "Are we at the end of the Protestant era?" Is there still a need for Protestantism as an independent movement, or could it be incorporated into the Roman Catholic Church, working as the leaven of reform within the church?

I believe that this question is becoming increasingly more difficult to answer. The consciousness of living in a crisis situation, an interim order, must be renewed within Protestantism, so we take nothing for granted. First, we must realize that the Roman Catholic Church is not the same unreformed church she was in Luther's time. We cannot be sure that Luther, were he living within the conditions of present-day Catholicism, would sound his call to reform in the same uncompromising fashion, especially if he knew that his Reformation would turn out so many kinds of Protestants. If Luther had our historical hindsight, he would see a Protestantism enduring a number of transformations—an orthodoxy equally as scholastic in method as the one he rebelled against; a pietism breeding the same *Schwärmerei* as the leftwing reformers; a rationalism which numbed the voice of preaching; a romanticism that drowned theology in a nature mysticism; a liberalism that pictured Jesus as a social worker; a fundamentalism that always fought the fight of faith in the wrong place, at the wrong time, with the wrong methods; plus all the later variations of a neoorthodoxy, neofundamentalism, and neoliberalism. In the light of all these changes is there anything that could still justify a continued protest of the "protestant principle" in a separate ecclesiastical order? The answer is: Not if the Reformation call has been heard and heeded by Rome! Everything depends on what Rome does with the questions that the Reformation continues to address to her. As heirs of the Reformation, we must still address those questions. We must make it clear, however, that we are not intent on a separate existence no matter what happens. We must be true to the Reformation and its message for the sake of the evangelical and catholic treasures of the church.

Although the Roman Catholic Church is not the same unreformed church she was in Luther's time, the Council of Trent was not a truly evangelical and catholic response to the Reformation call. The First Vatican Council proceeded, against loud protests heard within the Church of Rome, to integrate the dogma of papal infallibility into the contents of the faith, making assent to it a requirement of salvation. With the escalation of Mariology, dogmatic finality was given to a disputed teaching, thus widening the gap between the Reformation and Rome.

Protestantism has the meandering history we have briefly sketched, flirting with every ism that has come along, not always asking what the ism could do for the gospel but only asking whether it was modern. In general, this has resulted in a depletion of evangelical and catholic substance. The Church of Rome went in the other direction, not turning outward to the isms of the secular culture but, instead, turning in upon itself. In general, this inbreeding resulted in a loss of catholicity through an overdevelopment of genetic characteristics peculiar to her own family.

The Protestant communities and the Roman Catholic Church are engaged in a fresh encounter with each other. During the first rounds we have been feeling each other out, throwing an occasional wild punch or simply beating the air—going through the motions of shadowboxing. Pope John XXIII and the Second Vatican Council accelerated the pace of the dialogue. Both sides have felt deeply the need for a new encounter; both sides freely admit the need for reform. Neither side can feel proud of its history, but on what basis should the new meeting take place? Skydsgaard made the suggestion: "The two may at least meet in a kind of a solidarity of sinfulness, and that is not always a poor place to meet, even for two churches."[8]

Basic Differences

Inevitably, as Protestants and Catholics meet again, they compare notes and establish the areas in which they agree and disagree. Some of the old favorite caricatures are shattered. The battle lines are not always drawn where Protestants and Catholics expected to have to draw them. What we thought were major differences have become minor, and quite new difficulties have cropped up to lengthen our agenda of unfinished business.

What is the core of the difference between Roman Catholicism and Lutheranism? What is the central difference that explains all the other peripheral differences? At the time of the Reformation it was thought to be the article of justification, namely, the question of salvation. This question was posed in individualistic ways: How can I, as a lost and condemned creature, be saved? Where do I find a gracious God? It was thought that Rome gave one answer and the Bible another. Luther, as an interpreter of the Bible, said we are saved by faith alone, and Rome taught that we are saved partly by faith and partly by good works. Today we are confronted by an embarrassing fact. Roman Catholic theologians deny that we are saved by grace plus works. Salvation comes exclusively by God's free and unmerited gift. Catholic theologians who have taught otherwise have been in error, and Luther was right, standing in a long line of witnesses, including both Augustine and Thomas Aquinas. Küng's book on justification seeks to establish that there is no important difference in the subject of justification that could justify our continued separation from the Roman Catholic Church.[9]

What this probably means is that the quest for the fundamental difference between Lutherans and Roman Catholics has shifted from soteriology to ecclesiology—the doctrine of the church. More specifically, the chief difference lies embedded in our different ways of understanding the relation between Jesus Christ and his church. On this difference hangs a whole series of differences which remain on the agenda of unfinished business. We will list them in the form of questions.

(*1*) Is the claim that the shift in focus from soteriology to ecclesiology one that will withstand closer scrutiny? Are we Lutherans wise to let the focus shift without resisting it? Is the question of salvation, in existential rather than mythological categories, still the most serious question that people are asking? Are the Reformation and Roman Catholic answers to this question really the same, despite the possibility of harmonizing the Reformation theses with the Roman Catholic tradition?

(*2*) Is a person's relation to Christ mediated by his or her relation to the church, or is his or her relation to the church mediated by his or her relation to Christ? That is a false alternative, but what significance is there in the fact that often when Lutherans speak of Christ, Roman Catholics speak of the church? Have Lutherans stressed too much the difference between Christ and the church and Roman Catholics stressed too much their identity? Do Lutherans speak with too much ease about the sinful church and Catholics speak with too much ease about the spotless holy church?

(*3*) Does either side understand the meaning of catholicity? Have Protestants spiritualized the idea of catholicity so that finally it has only to do with the sum total of individuals who are personally related to Jesus Christ? This misunderstanding places in the shadows such things as tradition, church discipline, dogma, ministry, and sacraments. Have Catholics subverted the meaning of catholicity by equating it with what is Roman?

Our common creeds do not say that we believe in one, holy Roman church. We must find out why it is that whenever the Roman Catholic theologian says catholic he means Roman Catholic. Is the church catholic to the extent that it is Roman? Does Roman mean papal? Does it mean Latin? What kind of category is Roman? Is it like the adjective Lutheran? But no right-minded Lutheran would think of saying that Lutheran and catholic are synonyms. We do not really know what *Roman* Catholic means. Connected with this question is the matter of how Rome thinks of non-Roman churches and non-Roman Christians? In some sense we are recognized as churches and Christians, but we do not yet know in what sense. Some Roman theologians have come up with the idea of degrees of membership in the Catholic Church.

(4) If evangelical catholics harbor the hope of reunion with Roman Catholics, they certainly do not and cannot mean *return* to the Roman Catholic Church qua Roman. The concept of return is inadequate simply because it suggests that Protestants are the prodigal wanderers who have to come home, while the Roman Catholic Church is the waiting father. There has been prodigality on both sides, and the Roman side has not been standing still. Furthermore, the concept of return, which grates upon Protestant nerves, does not reflect Pope John's admission that responsibility is divided, and that there is equal blame on both sides. The idea of a mutual advance converging upon the future fulfillment of what is valid on both sides is a better working hypothesis. It does not require either side to deny its own history, but, through further historical development, it allows for a future reconciliation.

(5) Could it be that, from the Protestant side, a sign of a development toward catholicity will be the recovery, including episcopal succession as a sign of continuity in the church, of the episcopal structure of the church? Lutheran theologians like Edmund Schlink and Peter Brunner of Heidelberg, my former teachers, agree that the historic episcopacy and papacy are important structures of the church catholic. Those who think this is a betrayal of the Lutheran confession should read Article 28 of the Augsburg Confession; they will find no order for a congregational democracy there. This article teaches that bishops *by divine right* have the power of jurisdiction to forgive sins, to judge doctrines, and to excommunicate. The Lutheran Confessions say that episcopal succession and the primacy of the bishop of Rome are strictly *by human right*, and not by divine right, but they are not, for that reason, unimportant or objectionable. Although not essential to the content of the gospel, they may be beneficial to the preaching of the gospel and the administration of the church. The Reformation protest against the abuse of these structures by the Church of Rome does not justify a permanent and absolute ideological opposition to every form of their use. On the ground of the necessity of the protest against abuse, it would be tragic if nonepiscopacy became a sign of the presence of the true church.

Whether the reintegration of episcopal structures would help to engineer a rapprochement with the Roman Catholic Church is quite beside the point. It should not be done for that reason, nor should it be done to make our ministry and sacraments more valid than they are. If it should be done at all, it must come as an inner conviction that, for the better ordering of the church and its mission, episcopacy is the answer to the atomistic fragmentation of Protestantism and is a gift to us from the wisdom gained through the catholic experience of the church in the East and the West.

The Church We Long For

The hope of reunion is not utopian; it is predicated on the knowledge that the sixteenth-century schism was a historical event and, as such, is susceptible of being superseded in the stream of history itself. We do not have to wait until doomsday. In fact, we must regard the suggestion of Karl Barth that the healing of the breach with the Roman Catholic Church will not take place on this side of *parousia* as a statement of resignation and despair. No one knows the shape of catholicity in a reunited church, but we are privileged in these critical and promising days to work for something much more glorious than anything we can now see. What propels us is not so much pride in what we do possess, but hope for what we might receive from the bounty of God's grace. We may quote the words of George Tyrrell of the Roman Catholic Church: "God will not ask us, 'What sort of church have you lived in?' but, 'What sort of church have you longed for?'" For our part, we long for a church that will be both evangelical and catholic, continuous with the faith of the apostles, and coterminous with all that is universally valid in the experience of Christ's body on earth. We long for a church in which all the members will be one with Christ and one with one another, even as the Son is one with the Father. We long for a church that will be one and catholic, so that the mission of Christ through his church unto all nations might be accomplished; unity and mission belong together. Let us work for the church we long for. Christ will accomplish his will, indeed, without our help, but we pray that he may accomplish it through us.

The Reunited Church of the Future

IN A CONTROVERSIAL EXCHANGE IN 1966, aptly termed by *The Christian Century* the "Braaten Brouhaha,"[1] I used a parable which likened Protestants to exiles.[2] From this parable it was possible for *The Christian Century* and others to infer that I was calling for Protestants to "return to Rome." One has to concede that the exile image, taken by itself, can lead to such an inference. After all, exiles do seek to return to their homeland. If Rome is equated with the homeland from which Protestants are in exile, nothing could be more clear than that I was calling Protestants to return to Rome. Home is Rome! In this light it would be most surprising if Protestants would not have let out a howl. Let's face it; no Protestant wants to return to Rome! Not only his head but also his stomach says "no" to that.

The parable, however, includes another motif which was completely overlooked. Before exiles can return to their homeland and be reunited with their fellow countrymen, a radical change in government must take place. As the exiles see it, they must struggle to overcome a false government—a tyrannical regime—in control of their fatherland. They think they are fighting and protesting to liberate their country and to be reconciled with their brethren. Ever since the Reformation, the symbol "Rome" has stood for false government in the Protestant mind. The parable has two sides that call into question the self-sufficient attitudes of both Protestants and Roman Catholics. To Protestants, it underscores the provisional character of their churches; Protestantism exists to become obsolete as an institutionalized protest movement.

Protestantism has yet to realize clearly its interim mission and the extreme abnormality of its separate existence. Exiles know that they live in a crisis situation, and they hope it is only temporary. They know that all is lost if they lose sight of the goal of ultimate reintegration of those who belong together. To Roman Catholics, the parable is a reminder that Protestants are still in exile and are not yet prepared to acknowledge Rome as their authority or the status it claims for itself in the church. Roman Catholics have the duty to create the conditions that will pave the way for the reunion of all Christians. Some of us hope that the de-Romanization of the Catholic Church will not mean its Protestantization. I do not believe that we advance one step toward reunion by Roman Catholics imitating Protestants, as if, in the whole range of Protestantism, one can find an attractive model of the church for the future.

The editor of *The Christian Century* rejected my parable of the exiles as an insult to Protestants, an invitation to suicide. He had a basic fact on his side. Protestants do not think of themselves as exiles. Instead, they think of themselves in terms of the imagery that *The Christian Century* editor proposed as more suitable, as emigrants from the old country to the new world.[3] The pilgrim fathers left Europe to build eventually a new nation on this land, eager to secure its independence in every way and to establish a permanently autonomous commonwealth. This is the land of the free and the home of the brave!

Protestants have cherished such illusions far too long to expect them to alter their self-image overnight. Americans do not seek to reunite with the British. It is absurd, then, to imagine that Protestants should seek reunion with Roman Catholic Christians in one church with papal and episcopal structures, on the one hand, and common creedal and cultic traditions on the other.

The image of Protestants as emigrants to a new land betrays a total misunderstanding of what the Reformation was all about; it contradicts the intentions of Martin Luther, John Calvin, and the other reformers. I will have to state again and again what seems banal: Luther never intended to emigrate out of the Roman Catholic Church and to found a new church of his very own. He hoped at most to reform the only church he ever knew, not to start a new one from scratch, like Joseph Smith or Mary Baker Eddy.

The Underdeveloped Doctrine of the Church

What we are experiencing at the present time is a profound struggle for
an adequate (true) doctrine of the church comparable to the centuries-
old conflict in the ancient church over the orthodox doctrines of the
Trinity and the God-manhood of Jesus Christ. What is rather surprising is that it has taken the church twenty centuries to come around to
the question of a true definition concerning itself.[4] Of course, I do not
suggest that the underdeveloped state of the doctrine of the church has
been a sign of weakness. It may well be, on the contrary, a symptom of
health. There is no dogmatic definition of the church in the New Testament; instead, we have a plurality of images that give flashes of insight
into the mystery of the church. A new ecclesiological dogma will not
constitute the church anymore than the trinitarian and christological
dogmas first created the Christian faith. Once there is a dispute, however, a clearly defined dogma becomes necessary. There were no ecclesiological heresies in ancient Christianity against which the church had
to define itself in strict terms. There is consequently no orthodox
dogma on the church in the classical-Christian tradition that can claim
to be authoritative. The mention of the church in the ecumenical
creeds was not motivated by polemical intent. The formula *una sancta
catholica et apostolica* was not contested by any heretical party in the
church, nor is it a formula that has been contested down to our own
day by any denomination or sect in Christendom. It is only when we
strive to go beyond the formula toward a dogmatically precise ecclesiology that we quickly reach the *aporia* that now prevails. The ecumenical
movement has foundered on the attempt to develop an overarching
conception of the church as the basis for unity. Since the Reformation,
all developments in the doctrine of the church have taken on a polemical nature. There are many ecclesiologies; in itself this raises no problem. Doctrinal pluralism may serve as a sign of the depth and the
fullness of the mystery of the church. Dogmatic uniformity may only
be evidence of rigor mortis in the ecclesial body. In this case, however, a
problem arises because our various ecclesiologies are contradictory.
They cannot all be true; their mutual exclusiveness prevents the unity
of the church in its world mission.

Up to Vatican II, most Roman Catholic theologians imagined that if there existed anywhere a dogmatically precise and fully developed concept of the church, it was in Roman Catholicism. There has been a lively debate on the doctrine of the church in recent Roman Catholic theology. The quest for the true nature of the church, its essential marks and functions, is now as much a subject of inquiry among Roman Catholic theologians as among Protestant theologians. Protestants, of course, have been used to flux and even chaos in doctrinal inquiry. This is the price they have had to pay for the freedom of radical questioning. They derive some comfort from the fact that more and more Roman Catholic theologians are willing to join in paying that price. Freedom of honest inquiry is a basic presupposition in reaching a consensus that will pioneer the way to a reunion of the churches.

In both Roman Catholic and Protestant theology, there is a search for the appropriate starting point for a doctrine of the church. In nineteenth-century Roman Catholic theology, the church was understood as the kingdom of God.[5] Even in some circles of Protestant thought there was a virtual identification of the church with the kingdom of God. Then came the studies of Johannes Weiss and Albert Schweitzer that demonstrated that the "kingdom of God" concept in the New Testament must be eschatologically conceived as the inbreaking of God's rule, not as an ecclesiastical society in history with its own hierarchical structure—analogous to the sovereign states of Western Europe. Under the impact of Pauline studies, the "body of Christ" concept was made the starting point of a new development in Roman Catholic ecclesiology. As Gustave Weigel states: "The result was war between those who used the kingdom of God concept as central and those who replaced it with the notion of the *soma tou Christou.*"[6] In this war it is obvious that Weigel was on the side of those who stressed the organic symbolism of the body rather than the political symbol of the kingdom. Catholic theology has moved fast. Weigel wrote in 1961, "Ecclesiology is my own specialization."[7] In this article, he attempts to bring both Protestant and Catholic readers up to date in the area of his specialization. He does not, however, go beyond Karl Adam's doctrine of the mystical body of Christ or beyond the papal encyclical *Mystici Corporis* (1943). His article ends by giving the impression that Catholic ecclesiology has finally settled on the body of Christ concept as the most adequate for Catholic ecclesiology. Nothing is said anywhere in the article about another war between those who use the body of Christ concept as central and those who think that the notion of the "people of God" offers the most adequate starting point.[8] I mention this fact only to point out that if Weigel, whose theological specialty was ecclesiology, was unaware in 1961 that the people of God concept was emerging in theology and was destined to play a crucial role in the *Dogmatic Constitution on the Church* of Vatican II, then this can hardly be more convincing evidence of the flux in current Catholic thinking on the church. In a few years Catholic theology has moved from the kingdom of God, to the body of Christ, and to the people of God as the symbol which best expresses her true identity. Each step was greeted by Protestant theologians as an advance. In Protestant theology, especially in the ecumenical movement, the biblical idea of the people of God also became central.

Something ironic, however, is happening. While there seems to be a moratorium of talk about the kingdom of God in Catholic ecclesiology, there is in Protestant theology a return to the kingdom of God concept as the right starting point for a doctrine of the church. In particular I have in mind the works by Jürgen Moltmann and Wolfhart Pannenberg.[9] They do not start with a doctrine of the church, then ask about the church's relation to the world and to the kingdom of God. Instead, they start with the idea of the kingdom of God in Jesus' preaching as the basis of the church. The direct implication of this is that there can be no church-centered thinking about the church. Even the people of God concept tends to suggest that the church might be a chosen people as an end in itself, instead of a provisional instrument in God's hand "to pioneer the future of the whole world."[10] Starting with the kingdom of God as the basis of the church, it is essential to drive through the world to reach the kingdom of God. There is no relation between the kingdom of God and the church that does not include the world. There is a universal element in the idea of the kingdom of God.

The church is not the kingdom of God but has a vocation, its divine election, under the kingdom of God to pave the way for the absolute future of mankind. Before Protestant theology could develop an ecclesiology on the basis of the idea of the kingdom of God, it had to break with the tradition which identified it with the church. When the kingdom of God concept has similarly been purged of the church-centric thinking that characterized Roman Catholic theology prior to Vatican II, Catholic theology will advance with Protestant theology toward a deeper eschatological vision of the church's reality and toward a clearer conception of the relationship between the kingdom of God and the church. The quest for a fully developed doctrine of the church can only be satisfied when theology is recast in an eschatological mold, when it thinks from the end toward the present, from the coming kingdom of God to the church by way of the world. The eschatological perspective can aid the churches in ridding themselves of a self-centeredness that is no more justifiable in a church body than in an individual person.[11]

The Structural Problem of the Church

Prior to Vatican II, there prevailed a consensus that rapprochement between the divided communions would be hardest to achieve on the doctrine of the church. Although this may still be the case, the chasm between Protestant and Roman theologians is no longer as wide and as unabridgeable as it once seemed. Pressures from biblical studies, on the one side, and from the modern world, on the other, combined to soften the rigidities that had evolved through centuries of polemics. The results of these pressures are evident in the *Constitution on the Church* of Vatican II. A chapter on the "People of God" was given a place of priority over the chapter "On the Hierarchy." This was symbolic of a fundamental conviction that the distinctions between clergy and laity fall within the one people of God, and that the hierarchy's place has to be spelled out in terms of its service and ministry to all the people for the sake of their mission to the world. It seems, however, that while the *Constitution* made a real breakthrough in its chapter on the "People of God," it became timid and traditionalist, reverting to standard images and rhetoric, in its characterization of the hierarchy. One might say that while the biblical mind was clearly at work in describing the "People of God," the Roman juridical mind supplanted it when speaking of the hierarchy. An opportunity was missed to conceive of the hierarchy in a way that radically followed Pope John's personal example of ministry as the most humble servant of servants.

The chapter "On the Hierarchy" was not read by Protestant theologians with any great surprise. It served, however, as a reminder that, in spite of all the distance theologians have traveled toward each other, there still is a long way to go. The structural problem of the church continues to be the major hurdle on the way to the reunion of the churches. In his book *The Church in the New Testament*, Rudolf Schnackenburg acknowledges that the

> decisive question (and the one which separates Catholic from Protestant scholars) is whether the Church of the new Covenant according to the will of God and the disposition of its founder Jesus Christ is in its earthly form to possess an articulated, graduated (hierarchical) order with certain organs empowered to rule, or whether the "holy people of God," as such, possesses all authority and the necessary order is produced by disposition of the Holy Spirit at any particular time, in whatever way this may find expression. To put the matter more briefly, is a definite fundamental order constitutive of the Church of Jesus Christ?[12]

It is far too simple, however, to say that Protestant theologians are internally united and together form a front of opposition to the Roman Catholic definition of the church as the people of God hierarchically constituted. There are many shades of opinions among non-Roman churches, and it is even doubtful that Roman theologians have yet achieved a fully developed consensus on the legitimating basis and function of the hierarchy. One might say that many churches remain suspended in a state of uncertainty between a democratic congregationalism and a hierarchical episcopalianism. Some communities regard the hierarchical order of the church as an inherent ingredient of the gospel of Christ; they have difficulty acknowledging the validity of any ministries outside of that order. The task of theology today is to find a way out of the stalemate that we have reached on the decisive questions of ecclesiastical office and apostolic succession.

The remainder of what I have to state will unfold in four simple, and perhaps paradoxical, theses: (1) the matter of the order of ecclesiastical office and the structure of the church is not essential to the content of the gospel; (2) the reunited church of the future will, nonetheless, necessarily include structures, both papal and episcopal, along with apostolic succession, that have become familiar to us in the Roman Church; (3) papal and episcopal structures will only be acceptable to Protestants, certainly to Lutherans, when they have been divested of every authoritarian feature, both in theory and practice; (4) the way toward reunion will be marked out only by the impact of a revived eschatological consciousness in the churches.

The Gospel and Church Order

Bishop James Pike was once attacked by certain conservative Anglo-Catholics for not regarding episcopal succession as essential for the validity of ministry and sacraments. He quipped back that while Episcopalians have apostolic succession, other churches seem to be having the apostolic success. To have apostolic success, it would seem that emphasis on evangelical truth must take priority over ecclesiastical unity, as important as unity is. A reunited church of the future that subordinates the truth of the gospel to the unity of the church would only set the stage for a new rupture as severe as the Reformation schism. Christian faith seeks unity in the truth of Christ and refuses to be indiscriminately joined with those who seek unity merely for the sake of convenience and who have become indifferent to the question of truth. The unity of the church is something that must derive from unity in truth. A visible continuity in the structure of the church is not sufficient compensation for any lack of unity in the gospel of Christ. Community can only be founded on unity of faith. The Roman Catholic Church understands this; apparently some Protestant communities in the ecumenical movement do not seem as clear about it. Consequently, in a certain sense we cannot create unity, we can only recognize it. How do we do that? We don't do it by looking at each other but by looking toward the gospel. If it is the same gospel we see, then the church is already one. The church needs only to express its oneness through structures that give movement to faith, hope, and love, and that drive to the world and through the world toward its future in God's coming kingdom.

If our primary accent is on the gospel, and if we understand the church to be a servant of this gospel for the sake of the world, then we must say that the church is truly and necessarily present where the gospel is being proclaimed in word and deed. We cannot turn this around to state that the gospel is truly and necessarily present when a church bears certain institutional marks and perpetuates itself through certain external functions. One has to remember, even in terms of Roman Catholic theology, that right orders do not necessarily result in proper functions; and that canonical structures do not prevent bishops and popes, anymore than priests and laity, from falling into heresy, creating schisms, lapsing into unbelief, and forsaking their calling to see over (*epi-scopus*) the truth of faith and the purity of the gospel preached to the nations. There is nothing automatic about the correlation between the order and the faith of the church.

Because differences of faith run deep, there lurks the temptation in the ecumenical movement to transcend or circumvent confessional issues and proceed straightaway to achieve the unity of the church on the level of a common order composed by compromise. If this common order conceals rather than reveals, suppresses rather than expresses the dimensions of faith in the gospel it is intended to serve, then this order becomes subversive of the church's mission. Only by concentrating on the gospel, only by facing squarely the question of the truth of the Christian faith, and only by seeking a common confessional understanding, can we hope to find our way out of the ecumenical dilemma.

These statements come as bad news to traditionally anticonfessional or anticreedal communities. A nonconfessional Christianity, however, has never existed, and, where it has been attempted, the community either peters out into an association not distinguishably Christian or soon begins to compose new confessions made worse by their differences from the ecumenical creeds and traditions of historic Christianity. There is a most urgent need in the ecumenical movement to emphasize that the unity of the church follows from a unity based on the truth of the gospel. This means that confessional norms are unavoidable; there is no faith without understanding. On the other hand, unity founded on the gospel must not lead to a doctrinal uniformitarianism, nor must it preclude the possibility of an indefinite number of theological schools that work on the basis of common loyalty to the catholic tradition.

Ecclesiastical Office and Apostolic Succession

The concentration on the gospel of Word and Sacrament as the basis of the true unity of the church does not minimize but accentuates the importance of a visible, external manifestation of church unity in concrete, historical structures. Because we are one, we must show it forth; if we are really divided, it is more honest not to indulge in pretension of unity through common structures. Protestantism ought to put an end to talk about unity in spiritualistic terms, as if the unity we have in Christ is an esoteric, invisible unity that defies expression through visible forms. The heresy of Docetism never confines itself to one locus of theology, namely Christology, but spreads like poison also into one's conception of the church. Concern for a visible form of unity is a concomitance of a historical faith embodied in a community whose eschatological mission to the world is to demonstrate the unity for which all humanity is destined in the kingdom of God. If the church is not visibly one in an unmistakable way, she obscures her reality as a provisional realization of the peace and unity, achieved with justice and freedom, that will exist in God's kingdom.

The reunited church of the future will choose wisely to continue both papal and episcopal offices, not because this is the only imaginable way for the church to perform its mission, but because these structures best serve as representative signs of the continuity of the church with Jesus Christ and the Apostles and may serve as special agencies to attend to the self-identity of the church through the discontinuities of the historical process. They may quite easily be justified as hermeneutical vehicles, along with others such as the canonical Scriptures, the councils of the church, its dogmatic decisions, and the rites of the liturgy. All of these hermeneutical vehicles must be concerned with the one task of transmitting the tradition of the gospel to every new generation of the people of God. Quite simply: whatever the papacy and episcopacy are supposed to do needs to be done. They are specialized forms of ministry to the people of God in history. The needs which originally gave rise to the papacy and episcopacy still exist. Special ecclesiastical offices and functions, which help the church to be truly one, holy, catholic, and apostolic, are still needed today.

An approach to the episcopal office and apostolic succession that transcends the typical juxtaposition of Catholic and Protestant argumentation must be found. A better historical grasp of primitive Christian origins has weakened the foundations on which both Protestants and Catholics have built their houses. First of all, the Catholic case for its papal and episcopal doctrines is lacking any direct and clear biblical foundations. Even if it can be shown from the later epistles of the New Testament that the apostolic office is passed on to successors through the laying on of hands, and that the nuclear form of the episcopal office is then already visible, there is still a great distance between this picture of the bishop's office in the New Testament and the later dogmas which have been built up around the office. In other words, the claim of the succession theory to be the exclusive guarantor of valid ministries and sacraments is not found in the New Testament. It is, rather, a result of the later struggles between orthodoxy and heresy, in particular the Gnostic heresy.

On the other hand, the Protestant case against the hierarchy of the church has been shaken by what Ernst Käsemann has called "early Catholicism" (*Frühkatholizismus*) in the New Testament.[13] The monarchical episcopacy is already clearly in evidence in Ignatius's letters and in 1 Clement. By the middle of the second century the episcopal office has definitely become universal and has crowded from the field other perhaps more primitive forms of the church, presbyterial and congregational. When the Reformation churches abandoned the episcopal structure, not always of their own will, they were breaking with a tradition that goes back too far to dismiss it as an erroneous later development in the church. Therefore, if either the Protestant or Catholic position appeals in a legalistic way to biblical proof texts or if either has the urge to discover a duplicate of its ideas in primitive Christianity, it will be embarrassed. The legalistic mind that must find biblical precedent, undergirded by a clearly enunciated *mandatum dei*, for ordering the church will be shattered on the reefs of historical understanding.

I believe that Protestants should presuppose now that the reunited church of the future will be equipped with a papal office and the college of bishops. The reunited church of the future will get on with the business, not only of reforming, but of transforming both institutions to catch up to modern needs and realities. The question is not Should there be a papacy and an episcopacy within—not outside or above—the one people of God, but for what purpose and on what basis do these institutions exist?

The Relativity of the Church

The doctrine of the succession of bishops is not prior to, apart from, or constitutive of the succession of the church as the people of God. Instead, the doctrine of succession of bishops presupposes the succession of the church and its faith, and exists to represent and promote it. The same thing can be said of the infallibility of the papacy; it is an infallibility only representatively for the whole church. What is really infallible is the promise of God by which the whole church lives daringly toward the future. When the church confesses its faith, whether it is speaking of its unity, holiness, catholicity, or apostolicity, it is certainly not boasting of itself. It is speaking of God's grace upon and within it. The same is true when the church confesses that God will not withdraw his persevering grace to keep the church unfailingly, that is infallibly, in its way as the representative of the kingdom of God in history.

When Protestants hear Catholics or the Pope speak of infallibility, it definitely sounds like boasting. It is not heard as a witness to the generosity of God's grace. What can Catholics do to change their way of speaking about infallibility? Leslie Dewart states:

> The doctrine of the infallibility of the magisterium of the Church, particularly in respect to the infallibility of the pope, would be misunderstood if one neglected the intrinsic reference of that infallibility to the faith of the Church. What is radically infallible is that faith. That is, we believe that the faith of the Church is privileged in that it shall not suffer ultimate failure, a privilege which, of course,

no individual believer ever has. . . . Essentially, it can only be the
assurance of the *ultimately* unfailing nature of the Christian faith in
and through the establishment of a legitimate teaching authority for
the benefit of the faith of the church as a whole. The "privilege" of
infallibility is thus essentially related to the *eschatological* nature of
the church as a *believing community*."[14]

The crucial word is "eschatological." An eschatological perspective
radicalizes the relativity of the church and makes it clear that infallibility cannot mean security, inerrancy, and omniscience. The church
travels in history under the sign of the cross in humility and service, not
in the "arrogance of power" and triumphal self-assurance.

Catholics today are involved in an authority crisis comparable to
the one that Protestants experienced when the infallibility of the Bible
was challenged by the findings of historical criticism. Protestant theologians at that time began an unfinished quest for a new understanding
of authority which shifted the meaning of their words about the
inspired, inerrant, revealed Word of God. In an age of historical consciousness, such things as infallible authorities, inerrant writings, or
absolute principles, have to come to mean something else, even though
the same words are used. A concept changes under the scrutiny of history. When scholars pointed out that the Scriptures are not, in fact,
without numerous contradictions, a self-torturing apologetic tried to
prove, in defense of the Word of God, that all the contradictions were
only apparent. When that battle was lost, theologians altered their own
outlook. Even when they still used words like infallible or inerrant, they
explained them in the sense that the Scriptures are trustworthy, reliable,
and perfect, but only with respect to their purpose as documents wit-
nessing from faith unto faith, as human records of divine revelation,
and as texts serving the ongoing proclamation of the church. A historical perspective became the occasion for new interpretations. Something
similar is surely happening among Roman Catholic theologians with
the traditional concepts of apostolic succession and papal infallibility.
Such concepts have to be tested, therefore, in the light of both the
eschatological and the historical relativity of the church.

The Anachronism of Authoritarianism

The convergence of eschatological and historical perspectives may teach us a few lessons. The structures of the church in primitive Christianity were culturally appropriate; they were not experienced as culturally anachronistic by either those already Christian or by the new converts. Structures in the church ran parallel to structures in society. Before one believed in the divine right of popes, one had already believed in the divine right of emperors. Before one believed in a verbally inspired New Testament, one already believed in a verbally inspired Old Testament. Life in the church followed the same grain as life in society. The church patterned itself after the political structures which were effective in general life. The structures that proved most appropriate to the conditions of life from the ancient world to the Enlightenment and to the French Revolution were authoritarian in character. At that time they were perhaps not thought of as authoritarian, but when the same structures exert their powers and claims in the same way today, a strong resentment is aroused in the human spirit.

Authoritarian structures, and especially their claims to rule by divine right from above (*ex sese*), are breaking down. First they broke down in secular society. The trinity of the French Revolution, *egalité, fraternité, liberté*, was quite naturally opposed, not only by the absolute monarchy, but also by the ecclesiastical powers. The spirit of autonomy was rising to attack all heteronomous structures. It would be only a question of time before that spirit would make its inroads into the church. The Reformation attack on the papacy and the elevation of the priesthood of all believers had prepared Protestants for an acceptance of the spirit of autonomy, and in some circles this spirit led to a thoroughly secularistic form of religious thought and life.

The "God is dead" theology is a symptom of this extreme trend. What this theology means essentially, I think, is that the spirit of autonomy is rebelling against a supernatural image of an authoritarian deity who is a threat to human freedom and responsibility, and who gives absolute commandments from on high that humans must obey for no other reason than that they have been delivered by an absolute authority. Such a picture of God is experienced by moderns as antihuman. For the sake of humanity, it is then said, God must die!

It is important to recognize that the spirit of autonomy is an attack on heteronomous forces, on authoritarian forms of power and control. The church ought to make clear that this attack is a justifiable expression of humanity's maturing sense of responsibility, freedom, and rationality; it is an expression of what Dietrich Bonhoeffer has called a "world come of age."[15] His expression, "*die mündige Welt*," implies that ours is a world in which each person with a "*Mund*" (a mouth) is expected to speak for himself or herself. That is a mark of "coming of age." The principle of no taxation without representation is now axiomatic in all political relationships in the United States. Decisions that are reached through processes from which people know they have been excluded have no power to bind their consciences and activate them. A renewal of the laity will necessarily involve a political dimension, otherwise the laity will be merely the unthinking servants or action groups of a superior brain trust. Mature, responsible people will not accept such a role for themselves in secular life. It would be foolhardy for the church to count on the loyalty and obedience of persons who do not participate in the political process of responsible decision making. We must hope that Karl Rahner is right in saying that Vatican II is only the beginning and not the end of the road to *aggiornamento*.

If someone should observe that ours is not yet a "world come of age," that large masses of people are still in a state of adolescent immaturity, still cannot think or speak responsibly for themselves, and must still be dependent on external authorities, the point has to be conceded. Does this mean, however, that the church, in making a case for its ideas, structures, and procedures, must necessarily presuppose the immaturity of people, thereby making room for itself only in the realms of human ignorance, weakness, and deficiency? If that is the case, then the church becomes reactionary and will seek to keep humanity in a state of infantile dependence. Consequently the church will lose those who have reached intellectual and moral maturity. Then the church becomes irrelevant for those who have "come of age." On the contrary, the church must always understand herself, not on the basis of the lowest common denominators in human experience, but in face of the superior examples of human development and achievement.

What I am saying is that structures of the church, like the papacy and episcopacy, will be very much needed in the reunited church of the future. In order to function as they ought in a "world come of age," these structures will have to be demythologized or de-ideologized. The structures will have to make their way in the modern world without *a priori* claims, without any advance billing subscribed by heaven. In an unprotestant sounding phrase, they must be justified by works alone, and not by faith. By their fruits we shall know them. They will have to take the lead in sacrificing all authoritarian features that are out of joint with the times. As the new eschatological community, in which the charismata of the Spirit are bestowed upon all and in which all are ordained through their baptism into Christ, the church can set aside all authoritarian forms which are obsolete in the new age. The authoritarian forms belong to the old age which is passing away. If the church is the representative of the kingdom of God in history, there should be political signs of the breakthrough of the new age. There must be leadership without authoritarianism, disciplined life without coerced obedience, unity without conformity, and freedom of inquiry without blind fideism. Then the church will be more true to her own Christonomous nature and, at the same time, will shed those cultural anachronisms which detract from her mission to the modern world.

Change in Eschatological Perspective

The changes, which Protestant and Roman Catholic communities require of each other to make way for the reunion of the churches, are not as great as the changes required of both by the demands of the modern world. Protestant communities tend to revert to authoritarian images of the church and its ministry, which derive from the past, as readily as Roman Catholics. The past hangs heavy on the churches. The churches know that they cannot do without their past, and their traditions. These traditions, however, easily become a prison rather than a liberating force. The church is tempted to identify herself with the past when the present makes radical changes imperative. The changes, however, that the churches require of each other—as they compare their existing differences and the changes which the modern world demands of all churches—are really very minor compared to the changes that are required of both the church and the world to make way for the coming of God's kingdom. If the church lives toward the future of God's coming kingdom, she will not only be open to change, but she will also become the revolutionary instrument of change. The question will not be whether to change, but only how to change. Change may result in regress as well as progress. Standing still is the stratagem of regressive tendencies. In a certain sense, *aggiornamento* is not enough. If the church asks how she shall change to keep up with the changing world, she will always be decades behind. It will always be a matter of too little too late. She will run fast only to stay behind. That is a damning image of the church. It betrays her eschatological calling to look ahead and to be ahead, to be God's vanguard in the world. The church cannot compete with the world in keeping up with change.

The church dare not make changing styles her new idol. Moving the ecclesiastical hemline up and down her legs may improve her looks in the fashion parade, but that has nothing to do with winning the "prize of the high calling."

What must the church do then to cope with the rapidity and plethora of change, if she cannot hope to keep up with every sort of change? She must revive her eschatological consciousness; that means to live in anticipation of the absolute change of the world in the future of God's kingdom. Keeping the picture of God's future kingdom before her eyes, she will issue her prophetic call for change. She will not glorify the status quo or any period in the past, for she will have a vivid vision of the great gap between the history of humanity to date and the future of humanity in a commonwealth of peace, unity, freedom, justice, and in an absolute fulfillment in communion with God. The eschatological perspective opens the church to the future and calls her to prepare for it. Thus, proposals for change that might sound radical if compared with the past or the present may appear quite mild or normal when compared with the future that God has promised for humanity. If God has promised the kind of future the New Testament proclaims, then Christians have the right and the duty to work for it. That means they will call for radical changes as approximations of that future, to prepare the world for it. Paul Tillich says, in speaking of the churches, "They feel—or should feel—that they are fighting agents of the kingdom of God, leading forces in the drive toward the fulfillment of history."[16]

It is both my hope and prediction that the movement toward the reunion of the churches will leap forward when all Christian communities take seriously their eschatological mission to the world, when all think of themselves not merely in terms of their past and not merely in terms of dialogue with contemporary culture, but all think back to their past and their present in light of that absolute future that God has promised and for which the church is called to prepare the world. For this mission, the church will need structures, as she has in the past. The most important question to ask, however, is not whether these structures will be true to the past—that is, our traditional ecumenical style—but whether they will open faith up to the future. For, in the day of God's judgment, the church will not be asked how successful she was in sticking to the past but how well she prepared humanity to be ready for the future of history in the kingdom of God. A new hermeneutic that is forged in the light of that future will level the differences in the present situation that prevent the unity of the church. It will be a hermeneutic that opens the eyes of the church to read the signs of the time on her missionary pilgrimage toward the end of history.

The structural problem of the church today will be resolved only through a transformation of perspective which argues for particular structures, not merely as extensions of the past, but as servants of the present and anticipations of the future. Our interconfessional conversations at the present time are to a great extent sterile because of an uncritically assumed methodology that debates the living issues of the present on the basis of dead ideologies of the past. While the past will command its due, a more adequate methodology will take account of the future orientation of the churches. We should not merely be asking about our agreements and disagreements in the past. Rather, we should be asking about our common aims and goals, about present means and future ends, and we should seek a disclosure of our unity on our way to a common future destiny.

CHAPTER THREE

The Kingdom of God and the Church

IN SPITE OF THE FACT that kings and kingdoms are out of fashion in the modern world, the theological scene has witnessed a reaffirmation of the biblical symbol of the kingdom of God. This is all the more surprising in view of the almost universally accepted requirement that for a religious symbol to be relevant it must be translated into language that is culturally significant. Because we are lacking the cultural context to facilitate a current understanding of kings and kingdoms, we are faced with a hermeneutical hiatus between the symbol itself and our life situation. The fact, however, that the symbol remains useful suggests that some of its original meaning breaks through the cultural barrier and speaks to the deepest concerns that people have today.

The symbol of the kingdom of God has surfaced with a new impact for a number of reasons. Two are most noteworthy. The first reason is that the ongoing crisis of Christian identity has drawn theology into an ever more radical inquiry into the origins of its history. This is the abiding meaning of the "quest for the historical Jesus." The result of this research is well established; Jesus of Nazareth proclaimed the gospel of the kingdom of God, calling for repentance and faith. In rebuilding the foundations of Christian faith, after the universal collapse of Constantinian orthodoxy, it has been necessary to get back to the original meaning of gospel, kingdom of God, repentance, and faith, and it has been necessary to interpret them in light of their original contexts. A controlling criterion has been the desire to remain faithful to the message of Jesus and to understand its inner connection with the christological kerygma. Adolf von Harnack formulated the problem: "Jesus preached the kingdom of God as good news, but the apostles preached the Lord Jesus Christ."[1] In striving for a solution to this problem, the notion of the kingdom of God has assumed a new importance in our theology. We cannot claim the kerygma of Jesus as Lord without going back to the gospel of the kingdom he preached.

The second reason has to do with the timeliness of the message of the kingdom of God in relation to the aggravations and aspirations released in the process of moving toward a "planetary totalization of human consciousness."[2] Something has been stirring within the life of humanity to accelerate the drive toward a highly complex social organism, composed of superconscious units of personalized existence. If something like this is happening at the present time, there is need for a religious symbol, both broad and deep enough to focus, to illuminate, and to make the process a signal of a transcendent future in the fullness of God. The kingdom of God may be just such a symbol. It is the most powerful symbol of hope in the religious and social history of humankind. It combines social, political, and personal dimensions of fulfillment; it unites spatial and temporal elements in an eschatological synthesis; it promises healing to bodily and spiritual illness, liberation from authoritarian bondage, justice for the oppressed, righteousness for sinners, and homecoming for exiles. The kingdom of God is a transcendent aggression against the demonic powers that rule in history and personal life.

The kingdom of God, being at the core of Jesus' preaching, gives foundation and content to the quest for Christian identity. It provides answers to the quest for total personal and communal fulfillment by offering a future in which love, power, and righteousness work in perfect harmony for the good of all. But there are other advantages. It takes up and carries forward the theme of the kingdom of God that was abruptly discontinued with the great influx of neoorthodox theology; it reestablishes continuity with an idea that is deeply ingrained in American experience. H. Richard Niebuhr, in his masterful way, wrote about the history of the idea of the kingdom of God in the workings of American history.[3] It is astonishing to discover that the great outbursts of religious enthusiasm and theological creativity in America are stimulated by belief in the coming kingdom of God. This religious faith also shines through cultural history. It is not far-fetched to say that American history from the beginning has been a pioneering movement, pushing back the frontiers to explore the realm of the future and to receive what the Lord has in store for his people.[4] The fact that this quasi-messianic dimension of American consciousness has recently been corrupted by the demonic powers of national haughtiness, of industrial greed, of military bloodthirstiness, and of ideological arrogance should not dissuade us from appreciating its positive contributions to Christianity in America.

In European theology a similar thing is happening. One Lutheran theologian was quoted as stating that "generally speaking contemporary Protestant theology in all its fields has lost the basic idea of Jesus' preaching."[5] He meant that the various crisis- and word-oriented theologies after World War I displaced the theme of the kingdom of God that had an illustrious history from Immanuel Kant through Albrecht Ritschl. Wolfhart Pannenberg states point blank that "the dogmatics of recent decades is marked by a steady erosion of the notion of the kingdom of God."[6] Thus, when systematic theology today recovers the centrality of the idea of the kingdom of God, it is reestablishing continuity with nineteenth-century theology that, not so long ago, was written off as a neo-Protestant heresy. In doing so, it offers an eschatological understanding of the kingdom as a corrective to the dominantly ethical model that prevailed in the Kant-Ritschl line of thought.

The most important thing about the new affirmation of the kingdom of God in theology is what it might mean for the renewal of the church. The organized church has become the religious honey on the honeycomb of our one-dimensional society. The church tends to serve as the religious function of society and is expected to act as one of its smooth-running parts, along with business, labor, government, education, and entertainment. To the extent to which this is so, the church has lost its power to mediate transcendence. Mediating the sense of transcendence is experienced in terms of prophetic aggression against the establishment of the status quo, overshooting the present by following the signals of hope, and heightening the existential sense of alienation under the conditions of history. The symbol of the kingdom of

God offers the church a horizon of transcendence, opening up a distance between the future of life it proclaims and the conditions of the present that resist its advent.

The Quest for an Adequate Eschatology

The struggle to regain a position of centrality for the kingdom of God in theology may be characterized as a quest for an adequate eschatology. A special problem of this quest has been how to handle the theme of the future. With the rediscovery, notably through the studies of Johannes Weiss and Albert Schweitzer, of the apocalyptic framework within which Jesus proclaimed the kingdom of God, the dimension of the future in the structure of Jesus' message has come more forcefully into its own. The kingdom of God is immediately at the door; it is an event very near but not yet altogether here. The power of this future has a present impact, to be sure, but it does not cease to hold open a temporal distance between what is already the case and what the future will bring. An eschatology that is not centered in the future is not genuine eschatology but may only be axiology (a theory of values) or mysticism.

Numerous attempts have been made to absorb the future into the present in some form of realized eschatology. The category of hope in the oncoming future of God has often been transposed to the experience of faith in his transcendental presence. Platonism once provided Christianity with the conceptual means to defuturize its own eschatology. In modern times this role has been played, first, by idealism, then, by its stepchild, existentialism. Eschatology then becomes the doctrine of the eternal shining through the presence of all being or through the existential moment. Then Christian faith may look upward, inward or backward; but the forward movement of hope, fired by the world-driving promise of God, is arrested on its way.

Karl Barth elevated the place of eschatology in Christianity when he stated, "Christianity that is not entirely and altogether eschatology has entirely and altogether nothing to do with Christ."[7] In the various theologies that were born under the spell of dialectical thought, the future never wholly drops out of sight. We shall try to trace out the fate of the future in the vise of the eternity/time dialectic and in the subjectivism of existentialist theology. Here and there, the theme of the future appears as an oasis in systems of thought that have otherwise defuturized eschatology.

Beginning with Barth, we can hazard some generalizations. There is no doubt that all parts of Barth's theology are threaded together by eschatology; it is only a question of what kind. As a theologian of crisis, Barth juxtaposed the world of the eternal God above to the world of humanity here below. Eschatology, which has to do with the future destiny of this world, is lifted into a transcendental realm above it. The eschatological event is the *nunc aeternitatis* that can only touch history at a tangent but cannot, itself, have a history. Eschatology lies outside of history, in a prehistory or a suprahistory. The history of Jesus Christ shrivels to a bare mathematical point as an eschatological event. The resurrection of Christ, for example, is called an eschatological event, and that supposedly means it cannot be a historical event. The *parousia* has nothing really to do with new events that hope expects from the future of God. It is swallowed up in the eschatological present of the eternal now. Eschatology is, thus, not a doctrine of the future—neither the future of humanity and its world, nor the future of God and his approaching kingdom. It is wholly absorbed into the transcendence and eternity of God, coming down vertically from above. The horizontal categories of history and the kingdom of God in the Bible are spiritualized into the beyond of eternity.

For a time Barth seems to have become more aware of the inadequacy of an eschatology that relocates the future of hope from ahead to above. In a number of essays, he tried to break out of a starkly abstract dialectic of eternity and time, thereby giving expression to hope for a real fulfillment in the future.[8] He said, "Not that the kingdom has come, but that it has drawn near is the meaning, after as well as before the appearance of Christ, of the word that the 'time is fulfilled' in Mark 1:15."[9] Here Barth glimpsed the function of eschatology to keep hope alive and the future open. It is this tension between the promise of the kingdom and its future fulfillment that drives the church and its mission of hope into the arena of world history.

In the end, Barth never wrote the volume on eschatology for his *Church Dogmatics*. It seemed that, as he approached it, there was nothing new for him to say that had not already been contained in the incarnational revelation. The future can only have noetic significance, bringing a fuller knowledge of the revelation in Christ. Eschatology does not deal with new events, only with the final unveiling of the accomplished revelation of God in Christ. Does this really give us an adequate eschatology? Does it properly spell out the relation between the horizon of the coming kingdom and the reality of the church? Tjarko Stadtland poses the relevant question: "For many it was painful that Barth declared that he no longer wished to write his eschatology (*Church Dogmatics*, vol. 5). But could he really do that from the starting point that was his?"[10]

Eschatology also holds a key position in Rudolf Bultmann's theological thought. It does not succeed, however, in breaking out of its confinement in existential futuricity. The idea of the priority of the future is expressed but only in Martin Heidegger's sense as "the primary phenomenon of primordial and authentic temporality."[11] Yet, in his book on Jesus, Bultmann did not suppress the futurist aspect of the kingdom of God. He clearly depicted Jesus' message as an eschatological gospel of the coming of God's kingdom. This kingdom is "a power which, although it is entirely future, wholly determines the present."[12] The pressure of the future bears down on the present moment, making it for me the "final hour."[13] In reaction to the nineteenth-century evolutionary view of the kingdom, Bultmann stated that the future kingdom is not the consummation of the creation, as if it were already there in germ from the very beginning. The end is not brought about through a mere seed that lies latent in the beginning.

The horizon of the future shaped most of Bultmann's basic concepts. This is a legacy that present-day theology would be prodigal to surrender. Thus, humans exist in radical openness to the future: bondage to sin is enslavement to the law of one's past; authentic existence is the openness of trust toward the future; faith is freedom from the past. Faith is essentially hope directed toward the future. Salvation is an ever-coming occurrence out of the future, to be grasped through faith alone. The grace of God is the power to assure the future as life, instead of the future as death.

Bultmann's quest for an adequate eschatology was hampered by his great dependence on existentialist philosophy. This means that the eschatological future of God's kingdom tends to be reduced to the element of bare futurity in the structure of time in human existence. Eschatology becomes scarcely more than the significance of the factor of futurity for the individual. The future, however, of eschatological hope must have a new basis in reality that transcends the futurity of existence. Why? Because death is the eschaton of existence as such. This new basis is understood by Christian faith to be the resurrection of Jesus of Nazareth. It is necessary to trespass the limits of existentialist analysis to speak of a future of existence that spells life rather than death. There is another crucial point. The future of the kingdom is not merely the hope of existence; it also embraces the future of the world, history, and human community. The eschatological future in the biblical kerygma is not reducible to existential futurity.

The ultimate ground for speaking of the future of existence and the future of the world must be located in a theontological doctrine of the future. God is the power of the absolute future. Bultmann's language concerning the future became impoverished by its existentialist reduction because it was not mounted on an adequate doctrine of the being of God within the horizon of biblical eschatology. So, finally, there is no way to prevent the future from being reduced to the ever-receding horizon of man's openness, without shape, content, power, or reality of its own. The power of the future is rendered sterile by being absorbed into the existential now, into the subjectivity of the self.

Paul Tillich made the greatest contribution, among the theological leaders of the last generation, to the interpretation of the doctrine of the kingdom of God. He defined the problem of eschatology as the question of the meaning and goal of history and, therefore, as the quest for the kingdom of God. The symbol of the kingdom of God has two sides—an inner-historical and a transhistorical side. The prophetic revolutionary aspect of Tillich's social thought drew its power from the dynamics of the kingdom of God in history. Tillich saw history as a movement in which the new is created, in which unique and unrepeatable events occur, and which runs toward a future goal. In plain terms, Tillich stated: "Christianity is essentially historical"[14] and "Biblical religion is eschatological."[15] This means that the Christian faith looks ahead for the future transformation of all reality, interprets the past and acts in the present in light of the future goal toward which history runs. The New Being is expected predominantly in a horizontal direction rather than a vertical one; there is an expectant hoping for the realization of the kingdom of God—the divine rule of peace, love, and righteousness in a new heaven and a new earth.

Paul Tillich's eschatological interpretation of history, however, did not win the undivided loyalty of his mind. It stood in tension with, perhaps even in contradiction to, the categories of his essentialist ontology. He introduced a suprahistorical ontology in order to overcome the antinomies of strictly historical thinking. The end result was that the problem of the future was solved by dissolving it into the permanent presence of eternal life. His notion of "essentialization"[16] works to translate the eschatological future into the mystical presence of being itself. Theological eschatology becomes a little wheel within the big wheel of a philosophical ontology. Essentialization bears a suspicious resemblance to the classic doctrine of the cycle of time in Neoplatonist philosophy in which the end is always like the beginning. The horizontal expectation of the kingdom of God takes a vertical leap into eternal life; the vision of the eschatological end curves back upon the ontologized myth of origins.

The final translation of the symbol of the kingdom of God into eternal life is the door that lets in the transcendental mysticism that deprives the future mode of being of its power and meaning. Tillich was right in striving to formulate a doctrine of transcendence. The question is whether Christianity has to borrow the categories of Neoplatonic mysticism to develop a doctrine of transcendence, or can it be more adequately achieved within a historico-eschatological framework?

It is doubtful that the conceptual difficulties we face in handling the idea of the future of the coming kingdom can be eased by shifting to the spatial symbolization of mysticism. In fact, by so doing, real transcendence is not achieved at all. Instead, it passes over into the immanence of the eternal now, which is understood as an ecstatic moment extending into its own depths.

The quest for a more adequate eschatology continued beyond Barth, Bultmann, and Tillich by the next generation of systematic theologians. Both Pannenberg and Jürgen Moltmann, whatever the differences between them, criticized an eschatology in which the horizon of the future is swallowed up by the eternal "blitzing" in from above. Dialectical theology did not think of eschatological hope as having anything to do with the concrete future. Future tenses were converted, as often as possible, into talk about the presence of the kingdom of God here and now.

According to Pannenberg, theology must accept Jesus' message of the kingdom of God as the basic starting point for Christology or the doctrine of salvation. He says, "This resounding motif of Jesus' message—the imminent kingdom of God—must be recovered as a key to the whole of Christian theology."[17] The kingdom of God is the eschatological future that God brings about. This is to be thought of as the power of the future determining the destiny of everything that exists. It is possible to call God eternal, not in the timeless sense of Plato and Parmenides, but in the sense that he is the future of our present and of every age that is past.

Moltmann also speaks of the future as a "new paradigm of transcendence."[18] This future is not to be thought of as the progress of the world developing out of the present. There is no transcendence in that. Rather, the future can be a paradigm of transcendence only by bringing into the present something qualitatively new. If we blow up the present into the future, without radical change in the foundations of personal and social reality, the power of evil is magnified along with the good. Consequently, our last state is not better than our first. The transcendent future is a power to attack the conditions of evil in the foundations of reality and to lead them forward through a process of revolutionary transformation. From within this conflicting and painful history, it is possible to project a transcendent future of history that is qualitatively other than just future history. A better future in history can be hoped for on the basis of the power emanating from the transcendent future of history that opens up new prospects and new possibilities.

The theological trends I have been tracing in Protestant theology also stimulated Roman Catholic theologians to rethink their own eschatology. Each of the great Protestant theologians—Barth,

Bultmann, and Tillich—attracted a significant number of Roman Catholic thinkers and left an indelible mark on their new constructions. As in Protestant theology, the trend to give a larger place to the concept of the kingdom of God, and especially to restore the dimension of futurity so essential to it, has its following in the sphere of Roman Catholic theology. Here we have the profoundest basis for new insights and new reflections on the theme of Christ and his Church. The eschatological perspective has the force of relativizing the traditional doctrinal differences between Protestant and Roman Catholic theologies.

The Eschatological Horizon
of the Church in History

I have given so much attention to the idea of the eschatological future of God's approaching kingdom because it forms the horizon for understanding the nature and mission of the church. Both Roman Catholic and Protestant theologies have had to reconsider the question of the proper starting point for developing a doctrine of the church. In the nineteenth century, there prevailed a tendency to identify the church with the kingdom of God. Roman Catholic theology conceived of the kingdom as a hierarchically structured church in history, analogous to the monarchies of western Europe. This juridical concept of the church was challenged by a resurgence of Pauline studies, which emphasize the mystical notion of the church as the body of Christ. This organic symbolism of the body proved, however, to offer too limited a grasp on the church's reality. It tended to be too static and ecclesiocentric, insufficiently oriented to the world and the future of the kingdom. With the beginning of Vatican II, Roman Catholic theology had moved on to appropriate a new symbol for the church, namely, as the people of God. This is the primary image that won its way into the *Dogmatic Constitution on the Church*.

The image of the church as the people of God is rooted in Yahweh's election of Israel in the old covenant. The idea of the chosen people is also an image that can curve in upon itself if it is not placed within the universal horizon of the kingdom of God. Consequently, it was a stroke of good fortune when Vatican II integrated the eschatological horizon into its reformulation of the doctrine of the church. We read, "The mystery of the holy church is manifest in her very foundation, for the Lord Jesus inaugurated her by preaching the good news, that is, the coming of God's Kingdom."[19] In an explanatory footnote of the American edition we have the further reassurance that "The kingdom of God, which Jesus inaugurated in his public life by his own preaching and by his very person, is not fully identical with the church. But since Pentecost the church has had the task of announcing and extending the kingdom here on earth, and in this way initiating in itself the final kingdom, which will be realized in glory at the end of time."[20] Here we have a common root for an understanding of the church today that both the church of the Reformation and the church of Rome can share: Jesus inaugurated the church by preaching the good news of God's coming kingdom. The mystery of the eschatological future is represented already in the very foundation of the church.

In response to the ecumenical situation today, and through reflection on the results of biblical scholarship, Lutherans are challenged to ask whether the definition of the church in Article VII of the Augsburg Confession is not too limited.[21] First of all, there is lacking in the definition any reference to the eschatological goal of the church, and, second, there is no mention of her essential missionary function in world history. If we are asking about the nature of the church, we cannot omit the fact that it is constituted essentially by its relationships, forward to the kingdom of God and outward to the world. If the church is a gathering of saints to hear the gospel and receive the sacraments, it is also a people on the move in history, pioneering the future of the world toward the fullness of the kingdom. As such, it is both a sacrament and an instrument, as Vatican II stated: a sacrament of the coming kingdom and an instrument for the salvation of humanity. The church is already a sign of the eschatological future it proclaims for the whole world. A doctrine of the church must be developed in terms of the tension between the kingdom of God and the world.

The widespread notion that the church is a voluntary association of persons who are united by a common experience may touch the reality of the church at the sociological level, but it is disastrous theologically. As a consequence of that sociological definition, it becomes difficult to overcome the idea that the church is a social club whose main purpose is to cultivate experiences that hold the group together. If the primary aim of the church is to generate and stimulate Christian experience, then the outward missionary thrust to the world will be felt as a risk to Christian identity and a source for the possible attenuation of its particular type of experiences. "Don't get mixed up with the world" is an attitude of mind that can exist even when Christ is placed at the center of the Christian fellowship. Christ is Lord of the church and the world, inasmuch as his universal Lordship possesses eschatological finality with respect to the totality of the created world. There is no way that the church can claim to possess a private relation to Jesus Christ that does not involve her in an outward thrust of mission to the world. To believe in Jesus as Savior and Lord is not merely a matter of having an I-thou relationship, it is more a matter of acknowledging him as the One through whom God's rule is being represented for the salvation of the world. To know Christ is to know God's intention for the world. To have faith in Jesus as Messiah implies an awareness of the dawning of the messianic age in the midst of worldly events. To believe in Jesus as God's representative is to have hope for the world—to believe that the world's future can participate in the victory of Christ's resurrection over death.

There has been a lot of talk in modern biblical theology about a realized eschatology. In recent years we have seen a swing away from that, stressing the fact that the future of the kingdom must retain its futural dimension in the very process of making a present impact. It never becomes a perfected, realized, or accomplished fact. It is important, however, to guard against a total surrender of the aspect of realization.

The claim of Christian faith is that the eschatological future of God has already arrived in Jesus of Nazareth, in his person, his ministry of word and deed, and in his passion, death, and resurrection. Its arrival in Jesus of Nazareth so futurizes his person through the resurrection that his life becomes our Christian future and the future of the world. On the basis of the presence of the future in Jesus Christ, the church becomes open to the future when Christ becomes really present in and through the church. To be open to the future is to share in the freedom that the gospel of Christ brings. In the church, the kingdom of God becomes actualized in faith, hope, and love. This is actualization through participation in the new reality of Christ. This participation is made possible by the proclamation, through Christ, of the good news of the kingdom of God and by the administration of the sacramental forms in and through which Christ is experienced as present in the community of believers.

Our doctrine of Word and Sacraments needs to be shaped by this eschatological perspective. Dogmatics cannot simply provide commentary on sixteenth-century confessional texts. A total recasting is necessary in light of the recovery of the eschatological horizon of authentic Christian faith. This recasting will disclose that, to the extent that the eschatological future of the kingdom is operative within the church, it becomes an anticipation of the new world that is being created through the dying of the old. Word and Sacraments are means by which the promised future is already being made present in faith, hope, and love. Christians can live from the power of the already—ahead of the times—because they live as though the end is now in force. The church is *simul iustus et peccator* until the rule of glory (*regnum gloriae*) because the eschatological righteousness it appropriates in faith reveals the sinful imperfections of its concrete life as a church.

The eschatological power of the gospel relativizes all the structures of the church and of its tradition. Nothing in and of the church can be exempt from the criticism that emanates from the eschatological word of God in the Christ-happening. The church, in history, meets every new situation with reference to the future already previewed in the coming of the crucified and risen Lord. The anticipation of this future reacts upon the church's traditional structures and keeps up the pressure from within. The overriding question must always be whether the structures of the church can still serve as sacraments and instruments of the coming kingdom of God. The mere fact that a given structure has a long history, that it can be traced back to the church fathers or so-called biblical times, is no sufficient warrant to retain it. Needless to say, the very authority of Scripture is not based on its antiquity. The authority of any structure in the church must be derived; it cannot be *ex sese*, a self-constituting authority. Even the best statements and institutions from the past are subject to the eschatological life and relative to the historical situation in which these forms must function.

A burning eschatological consciousness can shed new light on the structural problem of the church today. This problem still looms up as the major hurdle on the way to the reunion of the churches. On the one hand, we should not yield to a romanticism that blinks away the tough realities of our ecclesial divisions, and, on the other hand, we should not yield to a realism which is willing to say only what is politically feasible or convenient. The appeal to realism is often a way of escaping responsibility for the critical truth.

The church needs servants and signs of the union Christians have with Christ and the unity they hope to share with all humanity. The episcopal and Petrine offices, for example, can be affirmed by Lutherans under certain conditions.[22] Lutherans can even highly appreciate them for the services they have traditionally rendered in calling attention to the importance of apostolic succession, in caring for the unity of the church, and in symbolizing the catholicity of the vision. These offices remind the church of its historicality; it must not let its eschatological vision make it a fugitive from history. The church is called by the gospel to the front line of world history, to bring light to the nations, and, always, to seek better social embodiment of the coming kingdom. The church needs the kinds of offices that are a force for unity among believers, that send them forward into world mission, that tie their memories to the holy events on which the church is founded, and that signal a wonderful future in which all the separated believers on this wretched planet will enjoy a rendezvous in the kingdom of God. If the episcopacy and the Petrine office have been betrayed into captivity, causing them to no longer function in these many respects, then the thing to do is to liberate them. I think that is all that Luther wanted. He did not want to forget about those in captivity but to free them for effective service under the gospel. The matter, in this regard, is not different for all the other structures of the church. The process of reform and renewal is continually needed to reorient them away from their authoritarian features and, instead, reorient them toward the image of the servant and an evangelical concept of leadership. "Whoever would be great among you must be your servant, and whoever would be first among you must be slave of all (Mark 10:43b-44)."

The unity of the church can only be forged anew by putting the concern for the truth of the gospel ahead of the institutional structure of the church. A reunited church of the future, which would subordinate concern for a true preaching of the gospel to a form of organizational unity, could easily become the temple of Baal or the throne of the antichrist. The unity of the church cannot be guaranteed by the ecclesiastical office but only through a sharing in the movement of faith that was inaugurated by the history of Jesus Christ. The norm of truth that counts in the church is the scriptural witness to God's revelation in the person of Jesus Christ.

If the kingdom of God is the starting point for the church's self-definition, the church will not withdraw behind a wall of privatized religion, sealing itself off from the social and political realms of life. The question about the political relevance of the kingdom and the mission of the church in the social realm is very much disputed today in many churches. There has been a tendency for the church to involve itself in the public sphere at the upper levels, lobbying for special privileges and immunities. This alliance of the church with the upper crust of society, or at least with the relatively advantaged middle class, is having bad repercussions on the church's mission to minorities and subcultures. The church tends to be part of the established order, joining the fight for the status quo against the struggle for a new order. Where should the church stand in the polarization that sometimes occurs between tradition and innovation? Again, the perspective of the kingdom offers a guideline.

The Holy Spirit is the personal presence in the church of God's eschatological future in Christ. He is the Paraclete, the promised comforter. Can we deny that Christians have often appropriated the Paraclete to keep themselves comfortable in the establishment—as long as it favors them? The Spirit has often been invoked as a nonrevolutionary principle in the church, keeping it quiet and submissive. The church must be on guard lest the appeal to the Spirit becomes a way to keep Christians warm inside their ecclesiastical huddles.

The Spirit, rightly understood, is not a principle of comfort for those who have it made. He is the fire of the spiritual movement that is spreading around the world in the name of Christ and the chief source of inspiration in the advocacy of a world-transforming truth. Literally, *parakaleo* means "called to the side of." This suggests that we can think of the Spirit as the principle of one-sidedness, not the presider over the lukewarm middle. The Spirit calls people to one side, to take a side; this call can very well spell offense to the trustees of the establishment. In the history of the church, the Spirit has not only been the comfort of the conservatives but also the fire of the radicals. In retaliation, the ruling classes always erect a cross for those who threaten their positions of power and privilege. The Spirit is the defender of those who take up the cause of the Man who died on the cross outside the gate. Thus he became an outsider so that all those outside may be given a place inside the kingdom of God.

Permanent Tensions in the Doctrine of the Church

There are three ways that the church can distort its true nature, by reducing its self-understanding to a single pole of reference, either to the kingdom, the church, or the world. If the church commits the fallacy of reduction to the kingdom, it places all the fullness of the future against the emptiness of the present. It does not really get involved in the present, as it is a mere waiting room. All people have in the present is hope; the future has all the blessings. This life is written off as a bad mistake; the only thing it is good for is to make a decision to leave for another that comes in the hereafter. The picture is only a little less bleak when this life is thought of as only practicing, or getting ready, for something much more glorious in the future. This means that the past and the present are sacrificed for the future. There are eschatological sects that have betrayed this attitude. The reduction of spirituality to the kingdom can result in a sneer against creation, against the present time, against the body, against secular pursuits, and against feelings of joy and happiness that people can find in their daily vocation—in their friendships, their families, their aesthetic creativity, et cetera. This is the wrong way to relate the eschatological future to the past and the present. In the history of Jesus Christ, we are confronted with the paradigm of the sacrifice of the future for the sake of the present. The gifts of the Spirit are released into our life now; we can experience freedom now, peace now, joy now, and love now. We don't have to wait around for these qualities of eschatological life. On account of Christ and the outpouring of his Spirit, we can let the future be in the present.

The second fallacy is reduction of the church to itself. The word for it is ecclesiocentricity. The church exists out of itself and for itself. It controls the means of its own creation and perpetuation. The kingdom is so fully realized within the church that it has only to take stock of its past and live from its own precedents. It does not need to be open to the present or lean toward the future. It lives self-protectively, suspiciously, and defensively vis-à-vis the world. Perhaps it goes into the world to find new recruits, but, basically, it senses no solidarity with those outside its own walls. Everything that it is and has comes down from eternity and derives its justification supernaturally. It has the divinely appointed administerium, the apostolically founded magisterium, the dominically instituted sacramentalities, and the patristically established liturgies; with all this triumphal self-assurance, it squares off against the world. In terms of this model, the church's task is to hold the line or to restore the past. Its diagnosis of every ill is that modernists have changed the church to conform to the present culture. Faith is equated with fidelity to the tradition, not openness and trust toward God's future. The church's solution to the world's problems is for the world to listen to her; her solution to her own problems is to listen to her echoes in the past. The meaning of Vatican II can be seen as the attempt to correct this type of fallacy.

The third fallacy has been amply represented by the modern exponents of secular Christianity. The church is called to catch up to God's activity in the world. The world determines what is avant-garde, and the church, not wishing to be left behind, goes about trying to be relevant and with it. The church joins in a litany of self-condemnation coupled with exuberant praise of the virtues of humanists and all people of goodwill. In this reduction, the tradition of the church is sneered at as baggage, the Bible is honored as one of the classics in our Judeo-Christian culture, the structures of the church are only instruments for the improvement of society, and a Christian is a secular person celebrating the world come of age. Jesus of Nazareth is made to suffer what Henry Cadbury called "the peril of modernizing." The trend of *aggiornamento* in the modern church will surely bring about its demise if what is up-to-date is not criticized and relativized by the horizon of the world's eschatological future. The latest thing is as likely to be a tool of the demonic as of the divine power. God has no monopoly on action in the contemporary world. The antidivine powers have seldom had it so good because they hide behind the widespread illusion that this is a Christian culture. The secularist's fascination for the contemporary must not be equated with the Christian's anticipation of the qualitatively new reality that cuts into the present as a two-edged sword, bringing aggressive criticism and truth transcendent.

It has been said that we must retain the right order in speaking about the church, "that order is God-World-Church, not God-Church-World."[23] The mere switching of the positions of church and world in the series is unfortunate. What is the order in question? In traditional Lutheran terminology we could say that the world comes first in the order of creation, but, in the order of redemption, the church comes first. Such competition for priority doesn't accomplish anything. It is better to think and speak of the church as a special instrument God has created to lead the world forward to the kingdom of God. There is no competition between the church and the world. The church is the sacrament of the world's future; within its life appear the signals of the future, which the world, as well as the church, has in store for itself. The church lives, not a monological existence in relation to the world, but a dialogical existence in order to test everything that happens in relation to the future of truth that has been previewed in Jesus Christ. The church can learn from the world because God's kingdom is present to the world in a penultimate way, just as the church is present to the world as a prismatic reflection of its ultimate destiny.

In the revolution of faith and the institutionalization of the church, a twofold dilemma has accompanied the historical church from the beginning. First, how can faith be transmitted through the established structures of the church when it is only the Spirit that can create genuine faith, and the Spirit blows where and when he wills. Second, once faith is created, how can it go on living in the traditional institutions of the church without blowing them apart? The institutional church always tries to domesticate the living faith of its members, to create channels that can be planned, supervised, and recycled into the systems of the established church. When faith gets overly heated by the fire of the Spirit, the governing bureaucracy of the church tries to cool it down to room temperature.

The two leading traits of the institutional church since Constantine are state licensing, in one form or another, and infant baptism. Thus, the church has come to rely on the state and the state on the church in mutual cooperation. The state has even played the role of persecuting the dissenters within the church, before, during, and after the time of the Reformation. Infant baptism acquired the effect of discounting the need for the personal decision of faith. In reaction to this, there has arisen, in the underground church, the demand for strictly believers' baptism. The church is then composed of the nucleus of committed Christians, those who know whether and what they believe and the difference their beliefs ought to make in their styles of life. In the nature of this case, the church becomes a movement that goes counter to the worldly society. More than that, it also goes counter to the established form of Christianity that lives a hyphenated existence with the existing culture. The institutional church is seen as a monstrous accommodation of social religion. Being Christian and a good citizen come down to the same thing; birth and baptismal certificates are virtually interchangeable in this culture-Christianity.

From the viewpoint of the believers' church, the official church is always in danger of becoming the church of the antichrist when it exists in fusion with the dominant powers of the state and the approved patterns of culture.[24] The church is to be holy; this means to separate itself from the visible world in order to be a sign of the invisible world to come. The believers' church is a free community constituted by personal conversion and spiritual discipline. In contrast, the institutional church appears as a Judas-church. It is an organized system of religious works without true faith.

This is only half the story. The tragedy of the believers' church is that, in trying to transmit the faith of the first generation to the second and third generations, it is forced to improvise forms that bridge the generation gaps. With each passing generation the forms are maintained in the service of a diminishing content. The process of accommodation to make room in the fellowship for the lukewarm and half committed creeps into the believers' church, betraying the very signs of formalism it found so despicable in the established churches. Ironically, this becomes most evident in the handling of baptism. The first generation offers baptism to those who make a personal decision for Christ, and, by the third generation, it is decided that age thirteen is the right time to be baptized. What, then, counts as personal conversion is subject to considerable qualification.

Once the believers' church becomes established, it ends by becoming a shadow of the historic church from which it took its departure. In cutting itself off, it loses access to the great storehouse of tradition that the historic church has faithfully garnered with the treasures of faith. In time the sect will wind its way back to the mainstream of the church's tradition, or it will live alongside it in a parasitic way. The historic church attends to the ongoing process of transmitting the traditions of faith, preaching the words, writing the commentaries, remembering the events, commemorating the saints, and celebrating the liturgies. This process cannot guarantee the transmission of faith, but it still provides the occasions and stimuli that can lead to conversion.

The radical churches have been in hot pursuit of the kingdom. The heat and light they generate along the way have been of inestimable value to the historic churches. We could even say that established Christianity lives parasitically off the revolutions of radical faith that explode around her fringes. The sectarian movements in church history have often brought needed judgment and hope to decaying forms of official Christianity. There is a continuing need for the revolutions of radical faith, precisely for the sake of the survival and integrity of the institutional forms of Christianity.

Does the love of God, which has been revealed in the redemptive work of Jesus Christ and has been appropriated by the faith of the Christian church, have any relevance for the wider human community outside? Does the gospel of the coming kingdom of God make an impact for good in the wider social and political community? Modern anthropology has driven home the point that one cannot be truly human as an isolated individual; rather, one becomes a person in a universal network of social and political conditions shared with one's fellow human beings. A purely existentialist anthropology is an abstraction; a Christian doctrine of the human person must incorporate the sociopolitical dimensions of anthropology. If the gospel is for the whole person, then it must encompass the meaning of the social and political conditions of human existence. Is it any longer possible to hold back the revolution of love triggered by the gospel from entering the social sphere of human life? In the language of classical Lutheranism, is it possible to segregate the *regnum gratiae* from the *regnum potentiae* in a clean-cut dualism of two kingdoms? Are not both of these spheres of God's rule linked to the *regnum gloriae*, which is not so much an addendum to world history as the oncoming power of his rule that he presently exercises both in the church and the world?

The Lutheran doctrine of the two kingdoms, at least in the way it came to expression in the nineteenth century, has led to a static conception of the church and the world standing alongside each other, each one jealously guarding its own turf and refusing to be encroached upon by the other. At its best, this doctrine has worked to police the borders between the church and the world, and it has even encouraged harmony, cooperation, mutual goodwill, and functional interaction between the two. The essential eschatological basis of the social and political dimensions of the church's relation to the world, however, has not been adequately articulated in the traditional doctrine of the two kingdoms. It would at least have been better to have a doctrine of the three kingdoms, the *regnum potentiae*, the *regnum gratiae*, and the *regnum gloriae*. Even that would not help if they are kept undialectically outside each other.

Theological attention must be given to the fact that Lutherans in America, perhaps more than Lutherans in Europe, have become involved, not merely as citizens but as members of the church, with the issues that concern the entire human community. This is a new experience for Lutheran churches. For most of their history they have dealt with mainly internal questions, questions of doctrinal and parochial concern. Recently, a restless social consciousness has been aroused in the church, and Christians are developing a sense of responsibility for the world—its political, social, economic, and ecological well-being. Lay Christians and many pastors are demanding that their church bodies articulate pronouncements on social issues and promote concrete programs of service in the secular realm. In the Lutheran church, there has arisen an urgent quest for a theological legitimation of the investment of time, energy, and money in the public domain. Some feel that the church should stay out of politics and stick to the preaching of religion. Others feel that the beautiful rhetoric on Sunday is obscene if there is no practical payoff on Monday. Religious words must produce dividends in deeds.

The theological ethic that the church has operated with has been spoken of as "faith active in love." A living faith is expressed in loving service to the neighbor in the secular realm. This is the realm in which the phenomena of law and justice, reason and power, threats and punishments, hold sway. In regard to this realm, Lutherans have derived their theological position mostly from the doctrine of creation. In contrast to this realm of creation, there is the realm of redemption, which is based on God's saving work in Christ and realized on earth through the church's preaching of the gospel and the ministry of sacraments. In this realm, the phenomena of faith and love, joy and peace, and hope and freedom, prevail. The juxtaposing of creation and redemption can result in a dualistic antithesis, one in which the two realms are insufficiently linked to the eschatological goal of both the church and the world in the future of God's coming kingdom. The Lutheran stress on the two kingdoms has the merit of guarding against the dangers of either a Christianization of society by ecclesiastical heteronomy or a secularization of the church by legalizing the gospel. The church has no monopoly of insight and right action when it comes to the ways in which love is to be expressed through justice, justice through law, and law through power.

The rule of God's power in the secular realm also goes forward outside of the church's sphere of influence and, oftentimes, against its organized opposition. When this happens, it is a scandal of the church, and God's judgment will surely strike against the church for obstructing his will. When the church is behind the world in the struggle for more humanizing forms of social and political life, it has forgotten the total obedience expected of it in relation to the kingdom of God. It has forgotten that the gospel of the kingdom embraces the total person. The revolution of love released into the world by the preaching of the gospel cannot be confined to the inner life of the private individual but must extend its impact into the social sphere. Faith, active in love, needs to be supplemented by a love active in hope.

The fear of the social gospel that has gripped many Lutheran churches is correct insofar as it warns against the tendency to reduce the gospel to a mere means to improve society. The ultimate future of which the gospel speaks is then absorbed into the penultimate aims of a particular society. The gospel announces an ultimate horizon of fulfillment that overshoots all the objectifiable goals of the world's social and political orders. The gospel affirms the infinite value of the individual person in such a clear way that it withstands every effort to define an individual's worth solely in terms of his or her role in society or his or her contribution to the state. The gospel is the enemy of every totalitarian usurpation of the individual by society or its government. It holds out a promise of fulfillment that answers to the deeply personal longing to be an individual person, to be free, and just to be. For the sake of reinforcing the greatest possibilities of human flourishing, the church has the function to keep the revolution of hope alive. The symbols of human destiny in the kingdom of God, interlocked with the whole creation that is now experiencing the agony of its imperfection, inspire the imagination to hope for an ultrahuman fulfillment in the boundless being of God. The revolution of final hope does not postpone the outpouring of its regenerative force until the end of time. The final revolution, already now, enters into fusion with particular revolutions of hope for oppressed and alienated people. The master model of how hope for a final future can bring an infusion of hope into the present situation of desperate people is pictured for us in the story of Jesus Christ.

Eschatological hope functions also to relativize all social and political achievements; at their very best they are only partial and provisional signs of the future kingdom. The church keeps open the awareness of the distance between the better society we seek in the future and the ultimate kingdom that arrives from the future of God. This gives the future a prophetic realism; the church goads humans on to better forms of life without suffering the secular illusion that such utopias can be achieved apart from the apocalyptic intervention of God in judgment and grace.

What will the final future of life in the kingdom of God be like? The human condition is characterized by possibility limited by finitude. There is also a drive toward infinite freedom within humanity that seeks an unburdening from every limitation. Humans have an unquenchable thirst for the infinite. Augustine stated, "Man's heart is restless until it finds its rest in God." God is pure and unlimited freedom. Humans are not satisfied to stand still within the confines of finitude; they must go forward to new being and live from the unfettered source of freedom in God. Is the final goal of the kingdom to be thought of as a static finale to the dynamic struggle for freedom? Is humanity now in motion only to stand still in the end? Is there a final resting place—a mansion—to which everyone will retire from the struggles of life? If so, then the kingdom of God would resemble a Nirvana—an eschaton of nothingness.

It would be better to think of the kingdom of God as the power of the future which ceaselessly opens up new possibilities. The essence of God is the pure freedom that humans are seeking when they search for the truth and reality of their own identities. God is pure freedom because the reality he enjoys is underived freedom as such. The freedom humans seek is derived from beyond themselves, from the source of freedom in the future of God. The salvation humanity seeks, paradise, heaven, and eternal life, is not all peace and quiet. It is an ecstasy of life, a vital movement beyond every stasis. The symbol of the resurrection is just such an ecstasy of life beyond the stasis of death. The final Christian hope is to share in the victory of the resurrection and the life of our risen Lord.

CHAPTER FOUR

The Gospel and the Crisis of Authority

THERE IS A CRISIS OF AUTHORITY in the church today. The legitimacy of traditional authority structures has collapsed—whether that be the authority of the Scriptures, the authority of the creeds and confessions of the church, the authority of the ministerial offices of ordained leadership, or the authority of scholarship located in theological faculties. What has taken the place of traditional structures of authority is a process that substitutes power for authority. The breakdown of authority gives way to *Realpolitik.* Persons and groups that feel deprived look for redress of their grievances, not by persuasive argument or appeal to authority—authority that the whole church as a community of faith confesses—but by manipulating the levers of power to secure their rights. Elected officials, rather than conveying a word of authority inherent in the gospel, function as brokers of special interest groups. The result is fractionalism, mutual suspicion, and a kind of guerrilla warfare.

The idea of using quotas to establish the final authority in the church, of locating the place where the buck stops, was born in the trenches of power politics. It binds the decision-making of the church to a pragmatic concept of justice as the harmonizing of individualistic preferences and lifestyles. The church then becomes a photocopy of the multiple-option society. The rules of the games we play—in politics, the arts, music, food, recreation, and everything else—in the world are transposed into the life of the church with no changes. The authority of the Word in the power of the Spirit is displaced and gives way to the language games of power, law, justice, and rights. We need, of course, to learn these games for our day-to-day existence if we want to know what the score is. Are we being naive and romantic to expect more of the church? Should the church march to a different drummer? Is the biblical image of being in the world but not of the world relevant for the way we reach decisions about the doctrinal, spiritual, and moral responsibilities of the church? Should the heirs of the Old Testament prophets and the New Testament apostles do business modeled exactly on the discourse and practice of the Gentiles?

Authority and Freedom in the Church

The crisis of authority in the church is due in part to a backlash against authoritarianism. Whenever authorities cramp or confine the human spirit that is in quest of true freedom, protest and struggle are bound to erupt. This phenomenon touches all areas of life, say, between parents and children, management and labor, officeholders and voters, and so forth.

The history of Christianity began with conflict over authority. Jesus, our Lord, proclaimed the authoritative message of the sovereign rule of God against all religious and political powers-that-be that abuse their positions. "The sabbath was made for man, not man for the sabbath (Mark 2:27)." The apostle Paul had to defend the truth of the gospel against those who would imprison it within a legalistic strait-jacket. St. Augustine picked up the torch for the true authority of the gospel against Pelagianism, which would subject it to a human-based synthesis of free will and good works, and against Donatism, which binds the validity of the church's ministry and sacraments to the moral purity of its clergy. Authoritarianism as the abuse of legitimate authority is a part of the tale of church history. It happened in the case of Martin Luther when the authorities of Rome refused the call to reform the church by the standard of the apostolic gospel of Jesus Christ. It happened again when Galileo was silenced by the dogmatism of the Inquisition.

Surely the struggle for legitimate authority and the place for freedom in the church was the big story of Vatican II. A classic struggle unfolded between two opposing forces, between the reformation party and the restoration party, leaving the Roman Catholic Church still looking for a way between the Scylla of restrictive archaism and the Charybdis of destructive anarchy. There is no way for any church to escape the tension created by the need to return to the sources, *ad fontes*, which Father Yves Congar called "resourcement," and the need to be open to the modern world, to bring the church up-to-date, which Father Hans Küng expressed by the Italian term *aggiornamento*. Together with the Roman Catholic Church, Protestants are still fighting the battle for true authority in the church, a church that finds both its authority and its freedom in the original foundational gospel of the triune God that drives it forward in mission to the real world of today.

The quest for authentic authority in the church becomes more urgent in a time of crisis. Ever since the Enlightenment, theology has been confronted with what Gotthold Ephraim Lessing called an "ugly broad ditch."[1] On the one side of the ditch are the contingent facts of biblical salvation history that form the basis and content of faith and, on the other side, are the universal truths of reason that can be discovered through scientific research and philosophical reflection. The crisis of authority means that if we ever had a bridge over the ditch between the Bible and modernity—faith and reason, church and culture, theology and philosophy—the pillars supporting that bridge have now collapsed. To use the language of Paul Tillich, a huge gap has opened up, setting heteronomous authority against the autonomous self, leaving no apparent way to lead us into a theonomous kind of authority that transcends the split between objectivism and subjectivism. Lessing exclaimed, "If anyone can help me over this ugly broad ditch, let him do it, I beg him, I adjure him. He will deserve a divine blessing from me."[2]

Luther's proposal for church renewal and reform appealed to an authority above that of the church itself. What was Luther's authority? Remember that Luther's authority was not Luther. What Luther said may be interesting, but it can never function as final arbiter. If we asked Luther, he would not say his authority was his reason, conscience, Germanic feeling for life, or his religious experience. Nor was his authority a corpus of ancient doctrines or a catalog of contemporary axioms.

Even if we said Luther's authority was the Bible or the Creeds, we still would not have adequately identified what counted as ultimate authority for Luther.

What we are looking for is the absolutely reliable referee on matters of faith and life. Of course, we must begin with the fact that all Christians, whether Orthodox, Roman Catholic, Lutheran or Protestant, confess that God possesses absolute and final authority. Where does God hold court? They will all point further to Jesus Christ as the one in whom God is manifest and knowable in a supreme, unique, and unsurpassable manner. Jesus Christ is our Lord, the real authority in our faith and life. They will all say that, except, perhaps, a few modern heretics who call into question the uniqueness, finality, and universal significance of Jesus Christ. Beyond this preliminary agreement, there are different models of authority in the church. The questions are: Who knows the will of God? Who knows the mind of Christ? Who has the gift of the Spirit to declare what is true and binding for the church today? Where do we have the trustworthy medium of the self-giving activity of the triune God? Where do we hear the invincible word of the living Lord?

The Pre-Vatican II
Roman Catholic Model of Authority

At the Second Vatican Council, a shift of paradigm occurred in how many Roman Catholic theologians conceived of authority. We are using the word paradigm analogous to Thomas Kuhn's definition in his modern classic, *The Structure of Scientific Revolutions.* He says, "A paradigm is an entire constellation of beliefs, values, techniques, and so on shared by members of a given community."[3] This definition is close to the meaning of the word when people speak of the post-modern paradigm. This means that a shift has taken place in the consciousness and practice of people, in the way problems are defined and solutions are sought. Similarly, in Roman Catholic theology, a shift took place at Vatican II.

According to Kuhn, a shift in paradigm comes about over a lot of dead bodies. It is something going on over an extended period of time and, at first, only a small group of people are aware of it. The shift begins with the recognition of some anomaly. An anomaly is some kind of phenomenon that does not fit into the existing paradigm shared by a given community. When the anomaly is first observed, and it won't go away, people get nervous. They experience a growing state of disorientation and distress. The old paradigm is like the air we breathe. We take it for granted; we don't even think about breathing until the air is foul and we're bothered by the stench. People stick with the old paradigm until they experience something like a conversion, a change of consciousness. Once the Copernican revolution happened, there was no going back to the old Ptolemaic picture of the universe, no matter how much weight the church authorities threw against it.

Roman Catholicism seemed to have a solid workable model of authority prior to Vatican II, but a revolution was under way, at least among a few important theologians who saw that the modern consciousness of history and the factor of pluralism did not fit the old model. Vatican II witnessed a conflict of paradigms, but most of it happened behind the scenes in the drafting of documents. The old paradigm was shaped like a pyramid. The sociopolitical structure of the church was like that of a kingdom with a monarch as the supreme ruler at the top of the pyramid. Other authorities in this supernatural society are subordinate and derive their authority from above.

The church, in this paradigm, has a very clear set of hierarchical relations—of the people to the priests, the priests to the bishops, the bishops to the pope, the pope to Christ, and Christ to God the Father—so that the peak of the authority in the church pierces the very vault of heaven itself. There is unity, universality, order, and stability in this picture of authority. Who would want to change it? But then there are those irksome anomalies. With the rise of historical consciousness, change itself enters the picture and with it enter uncertainty, probability, and open-endedness.

The shift in paradigm brings about a change in the concept of truth itself—the truth of revelation. The old paradigm held to a deposit model of revelation. The truths of revelation were given as complete, unified, consistent, absolute, and immutable from the beginning. The truths are to be found deposited in the biblical bank of revelation. Truth is immutable. Just as God cannot change, neither can truth. If something was ever true, it must always be true. This was the Scholastic or neo-Scholastic paradigm that survived until Vatican II and is still holding its own in some places.

In this model of authority, there is no ugly broad ditch. Heaven and earth are united in the very structure of the church. The eternal and immutable truths in the divine mind have been deposited on earth by revelation and are preserved and proclaimed by the infallible teaching office of the church. Infallibility follows from the immutability of truths and essences. The ideal type of knowledge of truth is to know with certainty, to the exclusion of doubt, and the only way that certainty can be attained is by relying on an infallible authority.

Current Roman Catholic theologians do not explicitly appeal to this old model of authority. Theologians such as Karl Rahner, Hans Küng, Johann-Baptist Metz, Bernard Lonergan, Walter Kasper, Edward Schillebeeckx, David Tracy, Avery Dulles, Gregory Baum, Gustavo Gutiérrez, Jon Sobrino, Leonardo Boff, and Jon Segundo participated in a post-Vatican II paradigm shift, and they have found themselves, more and more, standing and staring at the ugly broad ditch, shoulder to shoulder with their Protestant confreres. A crisis of authority has set in. The polls indicate that Roman Catholics are all over the map in their beliefs just like Protestants. The revolt of Roman Catholic masses against what their established authorities teach about doctrines and ethics is catching up to the chaotic diversity within Protestantism. Roman Catholics and Protestants are feeling more at home with each other, sharing the crisis of authority in the church. There's a saying that expresses the feeling of liberal Protestants: "The only good Catholic is a bad Catholic." Misery likes company.

Biblicism and Historical Criticism

Protestant Scholasticism also functioned with a deposit model of revelation. This model has survived in the modern world in American fundamentalism. The Bible took the place of the Pope in guaranteeing the unity of divine immutable truth and the infallibility of its earthly medium. The Bible had to be as infallible as the Pope in order to secure the needed certainty for salvation. Wherever this view prevails, we are talking about biblicism. Biblicism is still the position of a major part of American Protestantism. Biblicism holds that the Bible is the final authority in matters of faith and life, not solely because it proclaims the saving gospel of Jesus Christ, but rather because all the words have been written down by inspired authors. Not only were they personally inspired by the Holy Spirit, but their very words and ideas were also guaranteed free of error by the controlling power of the Spirit. This is what is meant by plenary verbal inspiration, a doctrine still regarded by a sizable number of Protestants as the only answer to the crisis of authority. The theory of verbal inspiration vouches for the absolute reliability of the Bible on all matters that relate to cosmology, biology, psychology, geography, chronology, and history. In other words, the Scriptures are authoritative not solely because they declare a saving message of God's will through Jesus Christ, but because they give us infallible information on all the topics they happen to address.

Biblicism is a Protestant variant of the old Scholastic paradigm that could not meet the challenge of the anomalies that appeared with the modern historical-critical study of the Bible. With the collapse of the old Scholastic model of biblical authority, it was hoped that the historical-critical method could reach back behind the texts to establish the real historical events, to reconstruct what really happened. Historicism became the successor of biblicism. It became the dominant approach in the academy, but, today, it is widely recognized that historicism can offer no solution to the crisis of authority in the church. The historical-critical method can, of course, be used by friends or foes of the biblical message. The friends intended to use the method to determine more precisely what the biblical text actually said and what it originally meant, in order to prepare a better interpretation of the Bible for the modern world. The historical-critical method, however, has taken a strange turn and has now become an ideological tool used by biblical interpreters to make the texts speak in conformity with an assortment of hermeneutical options, liberationist, feminist, Marxist, ecological, structuralist, deconstructionist, new age spirituality, and so forth. The result is that the Bible has no objective truth or meaning of its own to speak to the modern world. Hermeneutical theories have strangled the voice of Scripture and thwarted its authority in the church and in theology today. In the old paradigm, the dogmaticians ruled the roost; they were the ones asked to deliver the authoritative judgments regarding the truths of Christian faith. In the new paradigm, the mantle of authority passed to the historical critics. At first they searched for the facts behind the texts, but that became nothing but an excuse to import their own meanings into the texts. The quest of the historical Jesus, as recounted by Albert Schweitzer, makes this abundantly clear and nothing has fundamentally changed in the meantime to reverse his verdict. Each biographer poured his own ideas about religion and morality into his version of the life and teachings of Jesus. The new books on Jesus, by John Dominic Crossan or Marcus Borg, are just as tendentious and determined by modern ideology as the old ones. Jesus is portrayed now as a proletariat, a Marxist revolutionary, a freedom fighter, a feminist, a new age mystic, and an apocalyptic visionary. All portrayals reveal more about the way the authors think than the way Jesus really was.

It is well known that no historian approaches the texts with a blank mind; every historian begins with certain assumptions and canons of research. Each historian has a certain worldview, an anthropology, and some prior notions about religious and ethical matters. The whole historical-critical procedure, for whatever else it's worth, has provided the church with no solution to its crisis of authority. It has brought the church to an impasse. Scholars seemingly cannot live without it, but its massive results are mostly inert and useless. In digging for the facts behind the texts, historical-critical reconstruction has tried to substitute its own interpretations for the plain sense of Scripture and has placed them against the subsequent churchly reading of the texts in their dogmatic and liturgical context. No one could make a case that sermons, preached under the strict controls of the historical-critical method and all its subsets, offer a clearer proclamation of the gospel than otherwise.

The Retreat to Confessionalism

The relativization of biblical authority by the historical-critical method has led some to retreat into a kind of confessionalism. If the Bible is unclear and historical criticism gets us no closer to its unassailable eternal truth, then some people think that they can retreat into a mighty fortress in their own denominational book of confessions. The confessions of each particular tradition are given the status of final arbiter. Some Lutheran dogmaticians insisted on the complete inerrancy of the *Book of Concord,* immune from all errors, even incidental mistakes like misquotations of Scripture. The old paradigm of absolute authority deposited in an ancient book continues in Lutheran confessionalism. It is the twin sister of biblicism. Pastors in some Lutheran territories were required to swear, without any reservations, that they would teach everything in the confessions as the pure teachings of the word of God.

A rebirth of confessionalism is not the answer to the crisis of authority. It is part of the crisis itself. It functions, at best, as a provisional strategy for Christians during the tragic interim of their separation in a divided church. Our confessional doctrines are not the word of God; they are not the revelation as such. They are symbols that point to the revelation of God in Jesus Christ and are witnesses to the truth of the gospel. Doctrine is the echo of the word of God in the mind of the church. Doctrine is a kind of doxological answer of the church to the word that God gives to us through the preaching of the gospel. Creeds and confessions do not claim final authority for themselves, but point away from themselves to the Scriptures—especially to the Lord of the Scriptures. The *Epitome of the Formula of Concord* tells us: "Holy Scripture remains the only judge, rule, and norm according to which as the only touchstone, all doctrines should and must be understood and judged as good or evil, right or wrong."[4] All other writings, including the Lutheran symbols, "are not judges, as are the Holy Scriptures, but only a testimony and declaration of the faith, as to how at any time the Holy Scriptures have been understood and explained in the articles of controversy in the church of God by those then living, and how the opposite dogma was rejected and condemned." The point is that creeds and confessions have a very important hermeneutical function, as

signposts directing the church along the narrow road of faithful interpretation of the gospel.

The Mystical Way

The failure of the traditional models of authority in Roman Catholic
and Protestant Christianity has led to the triumph of experience in theology. When biblicism, historicism, and confessionalism fail to provide
the objective means of access to the final truth of God and fail to provide the hope of salvation under the conditions of the old paradigm,
people take refuge in the inner core of their own subjective experiences.
Mysticism comes back into play as a solution to the crisis of authority.
The motto of mysticism is: Go into your own soul. You will find God
immediately there—that is, unmediatedly in the depth of your soul, if
only you go deep enough. Personal salvation comes through transcendental meditation or mystical contemplation, and that is all the authority you will ever need. By a system of religious exercises or ascetical
practices and by abstract meditation and mental concentration, you
may reach the point of identity between God and your soul.

Today the category of experience, not the Bible, the church, the
sacraments, dogmas, or theology, becomes the magic key to unlock the
mystery at the heart of the universe. Mysticism is individualistic and
anticommunal. Mysticism is oriented upon the private interior self, not
upon the historical revelation of God in Jesus Christ *extra nos*.

Perhaps we need to offer a qualification at this point. There are
manifestly different types of mysticism. There is a Christ-centered mysticism, such as that of Bernard of Clairvaux, lived out within the sacramental life of the church. Still, the mystical experience, as such, does
not solve the problem of authority for the church. The mystical experience cannot provide guidelines for the corporate community for which
Jesus Christ is the head. Furthermore, the God of classical mysticism is
often not so much a personal Thou as an impersonal It. In any case, the
apostle Paul called the church the body of Christ. Each member of
the body experiences true fellowship with God, not by going into the
depths of one's private self, but by being in a relation of love and service
to others. All experience communion with God in Christ and with each

other at the same time. The movement of each self is not inward as much as it is outward; hands reach out, in fellowship with others, to receive the grace of God poured out for the world in Jesus Christ.

So where does that leave us with our crisis of authority? If the old models don't work anymore, is there a new one? Can we point to a way beyond the crisis?

A Perennial Paradigm

I will conclude with a sketch of how to construe the way authority works or should work within the Christian community. I have seven brief points.

(1) First of all, I believe that the church has been given a paradigm for all seasons, one that is perennially valid down through the centuries and across all cultural frontiers. It is manifest in faith and baptism, so that, no matter when or where one lives in space and time, neophytes leave their old identities and enter upon a new eschatological reality eternally grounded in the revelation of the triune God—Father, Son, and Holy Spirit. We need not look for a new paradigm for theology. The trinitarian paradigm of our classical Christian faith provides a continuing framework of Christian identity transcending the discontinuities of history and culture.

(2) The trinitarian paradigm is rooted and grounded in the gospel of our crucified and risen Lord Jesus Christ. The biblical narrative culminates in the gospel's identification of God in the entire story of Jesus' life, death, and resurrection. God is never more divine than when he becomes human, never more true to his inner being than when he loves the world in the gift of his own beloved Son Jesus Christ. Henceforth, we will not look for nonanthropomorphic ways of speaking of God. We will follow the logic of God incarnate in the person of Jesus as the linchpin of our answer to the quest for authority. God has a proper name; God's name is Father, Son, and Holy Spirit, and whoever calls upon some other name will have to be satisfied with the blessings that flow from some other deity than the God of the gospel of Jesus Christ.

(3) The perspective of a trinitarian paradigm discloses that, in the West, two unitarianisms have been fighting each other—a unitarianism

of the first article of the creed that led to deism and/or theism versus a
unitarianism of the second article of the creed that leads to Jesusology
and hero worship. The Holy Spirit, who is the unity of the Father and
the Son, drops out of sight. Without the activity of the Spirit, there is
no hermeneutical chain that connects us with the mystery of divine salvation in the Word made flesh. Without the Spirit, the Bible is just a
book of ancient texts and not the canon of holy Scripture. Without the
Spirit, the gospel is just a myth invented by the friends of Jesus who
were tired of fishing. Without the Spirit, the church is merely an association of like-minded people who gather to remember Jesus and who
pledge to do the best they can to imitate his actions in the world. Without the Spirit, the water is merely H_2O, the wine merely fermented
grape juice, and the bread usually tasteless and good for nothing. Without the quickening power of the Spirit, the words you proclaim next
Sunday will not become the living voice of the gospel but merely the
pious piffle of a somewhat earnest preacher. The Holy Spirit is the *sine
qua non* of recovering true authority in the church.

(4) The criterion of what the Spirit is doing in the church is the
revelation of God in Christ according to the Scriptures. The church
needs to recuperate its confidence in the authority of Scripture, whose
plain sense can be grasped by any lay Christian and does not need to be
deciphered by an elite corps of scholars. This plain sense will be apparent to those who believe in Christ and have received the Spirit's gift of
discernment within the life of the church. This is what Luther meant
by *was Christum treibet,* what conveys Christ, the very key to Luther's
biblical-theological hermeneutic and his way of reading and interpreting the Bible. It is a circular kind of hermeneutic. Luther said: "Neither
you nor I could ever know anything of Christ, or believe in him and
take him as our Lord, unless that were first offered to us and bestowed
on our hearts through the preaching of the gospel by the Holy Spirit. . . . And wherever there is not the preaching of Christ there is the
opposite spirit—the spirit of the anti-Christ. . . . For where Christ is
not preached, there is no Holy Spirit to create, call, and gather the
Christian Church, and outside it no one can come to the Lord Jesus
Christ."[5]

(5) Where there is no Spirit, there is no gospel. Where there is no

gospel, there is no church. Where there is no church, there is no canon of Scripture. Where there is no canon of Scripture, there is no gospel. Where there is no gospel, there is no Spirit. Where there is no Spirit, there is no church. Around and around we go in a hermeneutical circle that will never end until the eschaton.

Where is the circle broken today? Why doesn't the trinitarian paradigm, which holds the center in place and gives the circle its definitive shape, work?

We need to realize that the crisis of authority is intertwined with the two great schisms in Christendom—the eleventh-century schism between East and West and the sixteenth-century schism in the Western church. The unity of the church is based on the Trinity. St. Cyprian said, "the church is a people brought into unity from the unity of the Father, the Son, and the Holy Spirit."[6] Furthermore, the unity of the church exists for the mission, through the church and its ministries, of the triune God. Where the church is divided and its ministries remain unreconciled, the channels of authority get clogged, and, at best, we find ourselves improvising, as we have done since the Reformation, with ad hoc structures. The best our divided churches can hope to accomplish, at the present time, is to signal their desire to realign their ministries with those of the great historic churches through a mutual recognition of ministries in the interest of restoring eucharistic fellowship.[7] That remains the goal of the ecumenical movement.

(6) The authority of the Bible will always limp in a divided church because each of the churches can justify its confessional distinctiveness by appealing to Scripture. As Ernst Käsemann has said, "The New Testament canon does not, as such, constitute the foundation of the unity of the church. On the contrary . . . it provides the basis for the multiplicity of the confessions."[8] The multiplicity of confessions does not justify the multiplicity of divided churches, each one standing on its own confession. It was the one church that embraced a plurality of expressions of the one catholic faith. Pluralism of expression was built into the gospel from the beginning; the early church circulated four Gospels that eventually gained acceptance into the canon of the New Testament.

In my view, it is essential that Christians take seriously the notion of trajectory leading from the kerygma of primitive Christianity to the traditions of early catholicism, which includes a diversity of canonical starting points of its fuller expression. The catholic substance of the church cannot be reduced to the sheer datum of the gospel. The church, which the gospel created, expressed its identity through the discontinuities of history and culture by developing the canon of Scripture, the creeds of Trinity and Christology, the liturgy of Holy Communion, and the ministerial offices of bishops, presbyters, and deacons. Why should we pick and choose like a bunch of freethinking sectarians? All of these dimensions of the church's catholicity have been abused, not simply the ecclesiastical offices. All of them play a role in the field of forces that constitute the church's answer to the question of authority, and all of them need to be continually renewed by the evangelical criterion of justification by faith alone.

(7) If heirs of the Reformation can accept the biblical canon from the ancient church, as well as its ecumenical creeds and liturgies—without subjecting them to the guillotine of the *satis est* clause of Article VII of the Augsburg Confession—there is no good reason why they cannot accept the ministerial offices that the ancient church developed to serve the gospel on its missionary way. The traditional offices of church leadership, bishops, presbyters, and deacons, may have been bolstered by the historical fiction of an unbroken chain of succession linking them with Peter and the apostles, but that does not delegitimate them. We know that Moses did not write the Pentateuch. We know that Paul did not write the Pastoral Epistles. We know that the apostles of Christ did not write the Apostles' Creed. Such knowledge does not invalidate them as sacred and authoritative writings for today's church.

The offices of the church exist for the sake of the gospel's universal mission. The church needs to express oneness in relation to Christ among its members through sacramental and institutional structures that connect the whole with the parts in local, national, and global contexts. Of course, there are no guarantees. Bishops and popes, like pastors and laity, fall prey to heresy, create schisms and scandals, lapse into unbelief, and betray their callings to be true witnesses to the gospel. Because of abuses, many proposals to get rid of the offices exist. Some churches have gotten rid of the papal office and kept the rest. Some have gotten rid of the papal and episcopal offices and kept the rest. Some have gotten rid of all the ordained offices and kept only the laity because all of the offices have been abused. By the same argument, why not get rid of the laity, since many more of them have abused their calling? It is an *argumentum ad absurdum*. Abuses call for reform, not for repudiation. The Augsburg Confession, in Article XXVIII, calls for the reform of the episcopal office, not its elimination.

I see no need to reinvent the wheel in matters of church structure. The churches on the way to reunion would be wise to seek evangelical reform and renewal of the traditional ministries of the church, including their diaconal, presbyteral, episcopal, and Petrine forms. These structures may serve as representative signs of the continuity of the church with Jesus Christ and the apostles and also as special agencies to mediate the authority of the triune God through the Word and the Sacraments. They may be justified as hermeneutical vehicles, along with others such as the canonical Scriptures, the conciliar decrees of the church, and the liturgical rites. All such vehicles must be concerned with transmitting the tradition of the gospel to every new generation of believers.

We are now at the ecumenical crossroads. Only the future will tell if pursuing the directions I am advocating will contribute toward resolving the crisis of authority in the church.

CHAPTER FIVE

The Teaching Authority
of the Church

WE HAVE INHERITED no ecclesiological dogma from any of the ecumenical councils. The ancient church handed down definitive dogmas on the Trinity and Christology but none on the church. The twentieth century has witnessed a tremendous explosion of attempts to define precisely what in the world the church is. The Russian Orthodox theologian Georges Florovsky acknowledged that we have no precise definition of the church that can claim to possess dogmatic authority. He said, however, that the absence of definitions does not signify confusion about the experienced reality of the church. "One need not define what is absolutely self-evident. The church is more a reality which one lives than an object that one analyzes and studies. Father Serge Boulgakoff put it so well. 'Come and see: one can conceive of the church only through experience, by grace in sharing in its life.'"[1]

Models of the Church

In speaking about the problem of authority in the church, one faces the fact that no commonly accepted orthodox doctrine of the church exists. In dealing with the hierarchy of authorities in the church—such as Scripture, dogma, confession, and ordained ministry—there lies the deeper issue of the authority of the church. How we answer the question, What is the church? shapes our understanding of the authority of the church.

The spectrum of images and models of the church in contemporary theology is extremely wide.[2] In Roman Catholic theology, the church at various times has been understood as (1) the perfect society (Vatican I), (2) the mystical body of Christ (Johann Adam Möhler), (3) the people of God (Vatican II and Latin-American liberation theologians, Leonardo Boff and Gustavo Gutiérrez), and (4) the sacrament of salvation (Karl Rahner). In Eastern Orthodox theology, emphasis has been placed on the church as (1) the icon of the Trinity (Bruno Forte), (2) the eucharistic community (Florovsky's neopatristic theology), and (3) the communion of churches (John Zizioulas). In Protestantism, the church has been spoken of as (1) the communion of saints (Martin Luther), (2) creature of the word (Reformation theology), (3) the messianic community (Jürgen Moltmann), and (4) the prolepsis of the kingdom (Wolfhart Pannenberg). Recent feminist theology sees the early church as a discipleship community of equals (Elisabeth Schüssler Fiorenza).

Ecclesiology is pivotal for our understanding of how God is accomplishing his will in the world through Jesus Christ and his Holy Spirit. Lutheranism, itself, has had no particular doctrine of the church to pass on. All its nagging internal disagreements on the ordained ministry stem from basic differences in the area of ecclesiology. Conrad Bergendoff wrote: "In no area of doctrine has the Lutheran church in America had greater difficulty than in the matter of ministry."[3] A profound analysis would have traced the problem to competing views on the church. My experience while serving on a number of churchwide commissions studying the doctrine of the ministry within American Lutheranism has taught me that problems on ministry are symptomatic of deeper-lying issues in the area of ecclesiology. The responses from the various churches around the world to the ecumenical document, the Faith and Order Study on "Baptism, Eucharist & Ministry," show how their different and even contradictory views of the church come into play in their criticisms of the "Ministry" part, which many found to be too Orthodox or too Catholic. Some felt it wasn't Lutheran enough.

Kent Knutson, former president of the American Lutheran Church, wrote his doctoral dissertation, under Wilhelm Pauck at Union Theological Seminary, on "The Concept of the Church in

Contemporary Lutheranism." He demonstrated that Lutheranism has had no particular doctrine of the church to pass on. Knutson found four major competing doctrinal concepts, each quite different from the others: (1) the attempt of Francis Pieper to repristinate seventeenth-century Lutheran scholasticism in his *Christian Dogmatics,* which has been enormously influential in the Lutheran Church–Missouri Synod; (2) eighteenth-century Pietism, which shaped the dominant concept of the church among Norwegian Americans, stemming from Spener and Francke and spreading from Halle throughout Northern Europe and into America; (3) Swedish High Church theology represented by Nathan Söderblom—subsequently by Bishops Gustaf Aulén and Anders Nygren, but especially the theological faculty of Uppsala—which has been very influential among ecumenically oriented Lutherans; and (4) neo-Confessional Lutheranism, a movement represented in different ways by Werner Elert, Peter Brunner, and Edmund Schlink, which arose during the German church struggle.

Knutson showed that Pieper emphasized a supernatural concept of the church as an invisible reality, as the sum total of the elect, the *coetus electorum.* Pietists like Ole Hallesby of Norway emphasized that the church grows out of the religious experiences of individuals who seek each other out to form little communities. Knutson rightly detects here a primarily psychological concept of the church. The Lundensian theologians, Aulén and Nygren, emphasized an ontological concept of the church; the nature and being of the church are the body of Christ, the *corpus Christi,* which results in a virtual equation of Christ and the church. *Totus Christus, caput et corpus,* the whole Christ includes both head and body. The church is Christ because it is his body; Christ is the church because he is its head. This is a profound theological definition of the church in its deepest reality. The neo-Confessional Lutherans emphasized a dynamic concept of the church as the pilgrim people of God. Theologians like Brunner and Schlink were influenced by Karl Barth, biblical *Heilsgeschichte* theology, Luther research, the renewal of the liturgy, the ecumenical movement, and also their experiences of the church's struggle against the "German Christians" during the Nazi period. In some ways, I have been influenced by all of these movements and schools of thought.

It is noteworthy that Knutson chose not to deal with the evangelical catholic concept of the church represented in German High Church Lutheranism by Friedrich Heiler, the Berneuchen movement under the leadership of Wilhelm Staehlin, and Söderblom's idea of evangelical catholicity in Sweden. Elements of evangelical catholicism crossed the waters through the influence of Wilhelm Loehe, but also with Philip Schaff and John Nevin, the leaders of the Mercersburg theology. Why did Knutson ignore the evangelical catholics? First of all, he was expressing a regional bias. His roots were in the soil of Iowa and Minnesota pietistic Lutheranism; no historians or sociologists have described Iowa and Minnesota as exactly being hotbeds of evangelical catholicism. Secondly, he was expressing a value judgment. He said, "A question could be raised as to its right to be included in our definition of Lutheranism."[4] Thirdly, he had no personal knowledge of the evangelical catholic movement. He knew it had something to do with the renewal of the liturgy and sacramental practices, but many Midwest Lutherans have dismissed such things as romantic aestheticism, as a preoccupation with smells and bells. Furthermore, Knutson concluded that this minority voice "would not add materially to an understanding of the situation in world Lutheranism regarding the concept of the church." Knutson's typology is not faulty. What he failed to realize is that his fourth type—the ontological ecclesiology of the Swedish theologians, Aulén and Nygren—is substantially identical with that of the evangelical catholic movement.

An Evangelical Catholic View of Lutheran Identity

In the meantime, the case for an evangelical catholic understanding of Lutheran identity has been renewed in our time. George Lindbeck, a skilled practitioner of the art of typologising, points out that Lutherans divide into two camps on how to read Luther and the Reformation, with what frame of mind, and with what sorts of assumptions and questions. The two approaches are the constitutive versus the corrective view of the Reformation. The constitutive view tends to search the writings of Luther and/or the *Book of Concord* for answers to questions, which have arisen in the course of later Lutheran church history, about the church and its ministry. If there is a Lutheran question, there must also be a Lutheran answer, and where better to look for the authentic word than in the writings of Luther himself and the Confessions. Didn't Lutheranism begin with Luther? Therefore, he must hold the key to solving our problems.

A contrasting approach would read Luther's writings on the church in the context of his struggle to correct only what he found erroneous in the church at that time. After his falling out with Rome Luther found himself in an emergency situation where he had to improvise, to fly by the seat of his pants, to state that necessity knows no law. This corrective view of Luther's reforming intention would suggest that his writings, occasional and polemical as they were, do not deliver timeless answers to questions he never raised. The corrective reading of Luther assumes continuity of teaching with the mainstream of the Western Catholic tradition, except where Luther indicates that certain doctrinal and institutional developments are in open conflict with Scripture.

The difference between the constitutive and the corrective views underlies the pronounced disagreements among Lutheran theologians in America today. The evangelical catholic movement is clearly on the corrective side of the debate. The Reformers were not Protestants and did not, in any way, resemble modern Protestantism. Modern Protestantism is largely the outcome of the various reducing diets administered by four hundred years of scholasticism, pietism, rationalism, revivalism, romanticism, idealism, and historicism. Barth called modern Protestantism a heresy. It is not the legitimate heir of the Reformation. Ecclesiologically it has become the illegitimate offspring that, by almost every criterion of church doctrine and practice, exists in betrayal of the founding confessions and catechisms of the Reformers.

Knutson was right; the evangelical catholic voice is a minority. He was wrong to assert that it "would not add materially to an understanding of the situation in world Lutheranism regarding the concept of the church." Despite its minority status, it has continually challenged the Protestant self-understanding of Lutheranism. The term evangelical catholic is itself not new. I do not know with whom it originated. Söderblom used it when he recommended that the three main blocs of world Christianity be called Greek Catholic, Roman Catholic, and Evangelical Catholic. The word catholic, he argued, should not be reserved for any one church. After all, the word appears for a reason in the Apostles' Creed and the Nicene Creed that all orthodox Christians and churches confess.

Heiler wrote an article titled "The Catholic Movement in German Lutheranism." In it he traced the roots of the catholic elements in Lutheranism back to Luther himself. He wrote:

> It was not Luther's idea to set over against the ancient Catholic Church a new Protestant creation: he desired nothing more than that the old Church should experience an evangelical awakening and renewal, and that the gospel of the sovereign Grace of God should take its place at the centre of Christian preaching and piety. Luther and his friends wished, as they were never tired of emphasizing, to be and to remain Catholic."[5]

As evangelical catholics are often suspected of smuggling their catholic bias into their view of the Reformation, Lutherans should recall the concluding words of the Augsburg Confession: "We have introduced nothing, neither in doctrine nor in ceremonies, that is contrary to Scripture or to the catholic church."

Friedrich Schelling spelled out his own vision of an evangelical catholicism in the concluding lectures of a course he gave, "The Philosophy of Revelation." He inspired others to think of the Reformation, not as the end of the road, but as a transition to a future church modeled on the Gospel of John. In close affinity to Joachim de Fiore's three stages of church history, Schelling postulated three stages of church history. The first stage is the church of Peter, represented by early and medieval Catholicism; next is the church of Paul, initiated and epitomized by the Reformation; and both will be followed by the church of John, which will be a synthesis of Roman Catholicism and Protestantism. Schelling said: "If I were to build a church in our time, I would dedicate it to St. John. Sooner or later a church will be built which will unite the three princes among the apostles, for the last authority does not annul or exclude what has gone before, but transfigures and absorbs it."[6]

After World War I, a High Church movement emerged in

Germany that called for the restoration of episcopacy in apostolic succession, the celebration of Holy Communion as the central act of church worship, the return of private confession, the use of richer liturgical forms, as well as the establishment of religious brotherhoods. The movement founded the journal *Una Sancta* to foster relations between Lutheran and Roman Catholic Christians; it aimed to create a synthesis of Catholic dogma and worship with the Lutheran emphasis on justification through faith alone and in Christ alone. This movement stressed that evangelical and catholic are not contradictory terms, but blend harmoniously together to form a comprehensive vision of the one holy catholic church. I will leave it to historians to trace the trajectory of these ideas from Europe to North America, the influence of some of the leading personalities like Arthur Carl Piepkorn, and the role of various publications like *Una Sancta* and *The Bride of Christ* and their editors. In light of all this, we will surely have to admit that we are dealing with a minority voice crying in the wilderness of American Lutheranism, but one can hardly agree that it contributes nothing to an understanding of the nature of the church and its ministry.

Satis est Reductionism

The Lutheran Confessions do not give us a full doctrine of the church. The clearest statement is laid down in Article VII of the Augsburg Confession, which reads:

> It is also taught among us that one holy Christian church will be and remain forever. This is the assembly of all believers among whom the Gospel is preached in its purity and the holy sacraments are administered according to the Gospel. For it is sufficient for the true unity of the Christian church that the Gospel be preached in conformity with a pure understanding of it and that the sacraments be administered in accordance with the divine Word. It is not necessary for the true unity of the Christian church that ceremonies, instituted by men, should be observed uniformly in all places. It is as Paul says in Eph. 4:4,5, "There is one body and one Spirit, just as you were called to the one hope that belongs to your call, one Lord, one faith, one baptism."

Some confessional Lutherans have forged a hard and fast ecumenical principle out of the words "it is sufficient." I will refer to this ecumenical principle by two little Latin words, *satis est*. This principle has been invoked against the "Concordat of Agreement" between the Evangelical Lutheran Church in America and the Episcopal Church in the United States, which proposes "full communion" and a set of procedures by which Lutherans would recover the historic episcopate. Those opposing the Concordat do so as a matter of conscience, invoking the category of *status confessionis*, by which they mean that the integrity of the gospel is at stake, therefore potentially bringing about an occasion for schism and separation.

A proper interpretation of the *satis est* principle can unfold only within a comprehensive doctrine of the church. Neither Article VII nor the entire *Book of Concord* provides a full ecclesiology. We must remember that it was the purpose of the Confessions to deal with matters of faith in dispute and not to write a dogmatics textbook for the Reformation. Luther and Philip Melanchthon did not set out to write a new doctrine of the church. As the *Apology* says so succinctly: "We have not said anything new."[7]

Lutherans have traditionally claimed that, for the unity of the church, it is enough to have agreement on the gospel and the sacraments. If Lutherans should now reinstitute the historic episcopate, are they not conceding that something more than consensus on Word and Sacraments is necessary for the unity of the church? Would they not be guilty of elevating an *adiaphoron* (something nonessential) to the level of an essential mark of the church, thus contradicting their confessional *satis est* principle? Lutherans have prided themselves on making only matters of gospel and faith essential and claim, thereby, to offer the most attractive, workable proposal for the unity of the church to the rest of world Christianity. Other churches, by requiring acceptance of a particular church polity, whether papal, episcopal, presbyteral, or congregational, impose obstacles in the way of church unity that Lutherans do not. This is what Lutherans keep telling themselves, but it continues to fall on deaf ears. Why is not the gospel of justification by faith alone and the means of grace simply enough for the unity of the church? I will try to provide the best answer I have been able to come up with.

In hermeneutical theory, we know that, to understand something in particular, taking into account its context is decisively important. Unless you take into account the context of a word, sentence, paragraph, or document, you cannot interpret it correctly. What was the context of the *satis est* clause of Article VII? At that time congregations supporting Luther and the Reformation were being accused of ignoring traditional rites and ceremonies of the church. They pleaded that they should not be treated as heretics or as less-than-true Roman Catholics as long as they retained what is essential for the church to be the church, pure preaching of the gospel and right administration of the sacraments. Other ritual practices may be useful for edification and discipline, but they are *adiaphora*, not essential to produce the righteousness of justifying faith that avails before God. Here Article IV on justification comes powerfully into play. The Lutheran concern in Article VII is soteriology, what is essential to be reckoned as righteous before God, and not ecclesiology, what offices and structures the church needs for ordering and maintaining its institutional life and faith. There is nothing in Article VII of the Augsburg Confession or of the Apology to the Augsburg Confession that deals pro or con with the ministerial offices of the church. What is clear is that the stress on Word and Sacraments presupposes the ordered ministry of the church, without which there would be no such preaching of the gospel and administration of the sacraments. For these essential practices do not simply happen *in vacuo*.

Therefore, the common Lutheran polemic against the traditional threefold office of ministry—bishops, presbyters, and deacons—in light of the *satis est* principle is completely anachronistic. At the time Article VII was written, the church of which the Reformers were members was a church equipped with the threefold office. The Reformers did not make a move to dismantle it, to level it down to a single office, nor even to get rid of the papal office as such. If the confessors had wished to repudiate the ecclesiastical offices of ordained ministry, they would have made that their explicit target. Instead, they stuck to soteriological matters and cited abuses of the time. They addressed the widespread mistaken belief that a plethora of rites, ceremonies, and works imposed on the faithful were somehow productive of the righteousness of the heart pleasing to God. This does not mean that the Reformers did away with ceremonies, such as observing feast days. These ceremonies may contain a discipline that educates and instructs, but they are not what makes a person a Christian. To be a Christian, the only thing that really counts is the word communicated through preaching and sacraments. The Apology states: "The true unity of the church is not harmed by differences in rites instituted by men, although we like it when universal rites are observed for the sake of tranquillity. . . . The question is whether the observance of human traditions is an act of worship necessary for righteousness before God."[8]

It seems clear that the Lutheran dissenters to the "Concordat of Agreement" are aiming the arrow of *satis est* at the wrong target. It is not the offices of the church's ministry but the imposed ritual observances having to do with food, fasting, and feast days that demand more than necessary for keeping the church of Christ united. The concern of the Reformers was, first and foremost, soteriology not ecclesiology. What we see of their ecclesiology in the Confessional Writings is only the tip of the iceberg; the rest remained hidden and mostly presupposed. The full picture has to be constructed out of their other writings.

To reduce everything essential in the life and mission of the church to the bare bones of what makes for salvation has been called gospel reductionism. In this case, we may use Michael Root's term *satis est* reductionism. At Augsburg, the issue in controversy was whether the Lutheran party was placing itself beyond the limits of catholic orthodoxy so as to deserve condemnation. The crucial issue was how to prevent schism and excommunication. Today, the issue is vastly different. We are facing a multiplicity of churches, some of which have anathematized each other and condemned each other's doctrines. What is necessary to unite churches, which have never been in fellowship, may require agreement on a number of issues that Article VII did not envisage, and that are not, in fact, absolutely necessary for the church's preaching of salvation. Other partner churches do not question the validity of the Lutheran ministry with regard to the preaching of salvation. Certainly the Episcopal Church U.S.A. does not. As for the ordering of the historic ministries of the church, at a level below the ultimate question of the righteousness that makes people right with God, the sixteenth century tragically produced schisms that can only be over-come by a series of church-to-church actions, one of which includes restoring the historic episcopal succession wherever it was broken.

We can no longer pretend that agreement on the gospel and sacra-ments is sufficient for the life of the church in all its dimensions. A strict minimalist interpretation of the *satis est* would dispense with the notion that the ordained ministry is divinely instituted and is therefore of the *esse* of the church. If we were to continue such a reductionistic line of reasoning—presumably derived from the article of justification by faith alone—other elements of catholic orthodoxy would be in jeop-ardy. Not only the ordained ministry, but also the canon of Holy Scrip-ture, the Ecumenical Councils with their trinitarian and christological dogmas, as well as the confessional writings of the Reformation would fall to the ax of *satis est* reductionism. The same church that gave us the canon, creed, and cult also handed on the ministerial offices of bishop, presbyter, and deacon. If the ecclesiastical office has been abused and stands in need of reform, the same is always true of everything in the life of the church—*ecclesia semper reformanda.*

Orthodoxy and Heresy

Luther once composed a list of seven marks of the church. In addition to preaching, baptism, and holy communion, he stipulated the keys of Christian discipline and forgiveness, the offices of ministry, public wor-ship, and the cross, that is, the sufferings of believers for their faith. No doubt we could extend the list. The point I want to make is that Word and Sacraments, though most assuredly essential marks of the church catholic, are not the only marks. Not any old preaching, and not any old sort of sacraments will do. There must be, in addition, the autho-rized offices of ministry that discern and test whether the preaching of the gospel is pure and the sacraments are administered according to the gospel. There also must be doctrinal criteria by which discipline can be properly exercised in the church.

In the last generation, we have witnessed in American Christianity a free fall into doctrinal normlessness and liturgical adventurism.

THE TEACHING AUTHORITY OF THE CHURCH 93

Clearly, we are speaking about the necessity of dogma, the authority of pure doctrine, on the one hand, and the need for a supervisory office of discernment and discipline—the office of bishop—on the other hand. As Article XXVIII of the Augsburg Confession states: "According to divine right, it is the office of the bishop to preach the Gospel, forgive sins, judge doctrine and condemn doctrine that is contrary to the Gospel, and exclude from the Christian community the ungodly whose wicked conduct is manifest. . . . Parish ministers and churches are bound to be obedient to the bishops according to the saying of Christ in Luke 10:16, "Whoever hears you hears me."

What is the church to do when heresy threatens its faith and life? Heresy? Isn't that the way of witch-hunting? It's a scary word. Thomas Oden of Drew University has this to say about the sad state of theological education today: "The modern seminary has finally achieved a condition that has never prevailed in Christian history: heresy simply does not exist."[9] The reasons are that there is no concern for pure doctrine and no ecclesial authority to tell the difference or do anything about it.

We live in an age of relativism (there are no absolutes), pluralism (there are many ways of salvation), inclusivism (everything goes, no questions asked), and indifferentism (who cares?). Truth with a capital "T" has been dissolved into a slough of tiny tribal truths all of which are a function of personal taste and preference. To each his or her own! It is no longer dangerous to teach or preach heresy in the church or to write and publish heresy in the church press. Where there is no orthodoxy, there can be no heresy. Under the rubric of multiculturalism, everyone's -doxy is as good as anybody else's and must be taken seriously, for that is their way of expressing their religious experiences and feelings about God.

Walter Bauer in his famous book *Orthodoxy and Heresy in Earliest Christianity* defended the thesis that, in many regions, heresy was the original manifestation of Christianity.[10] He called into question the traditional view that heresies developed as deviations from orthodoxy. Bauer's thesis was: In the beginning was heresy, and only later by certain power moves did orthodoxy become dominant, wrapping itself in the myth that it is being faithful to the teachings of Christ and the apostles. Accordingly, the myth of orthodoxy is nothing but self-justifying propaganda used by church leaders to establish their power and control.

Helmut Koester, a Lutheran New Testament professor at Harvard Divinity School, has applied Bauer's thesis to the current theological situation. He says that the formation of the biblical canon in the early church was the work of sheer dogmatic prejudice. The borders between the New Testament and other literature of the time were artificially constructed by people in power—all white males, as we hear today—to secure their own interests. So Koester says, these old borders must be broken down. "The canon was the result of a deliberate attempt to exclude certain voices from the early period of Christianity: heretics, Marcionites, Gnosticism, Jewish Christians, perhaps also women. It is the responsibility of the New Testament scholar to help these voices to be heard again."[11]

St. Paul knew that heresies would afflict the life of the church. He wrote: "There must be heresies among you, that they which are approved may be made manifest among you (1 Cor. 11:19 KJV)." 2 Peter 2:1 reads: "There will be false teachers among you, who will secretly bring in destructive heresies." The New Testament writers were concerned about heresy. It is damnable, dangerous, and destructive. It breeds factions, divisions, and cliques of which there are no end in the church today.

Heresies come in different shapes and guises.[12]

(1) There is the reductionistic heresy, which tries to boil Christian faith down to a single principle, like No Creeds but Christ, or Justification by faith alone, or the historic episcopate, or papal infallibility.

(2) There is the opposite tendency, the maximalistic heresy, which makes some new theory or practice, like teetotalism, verbal inerrancy, or women's ordination, a matter of *status confessionis.*

(3) There is the syncretistic heresy, reflected in New Age Christianity, that mixes Asian and, sometimes, aboriginal beliefs and practices into Christian rituals.

(4) There is the displacement heresy, which exchanges what is central for what is peripheral, such as placing the politically correct libera-

tionist agendas of today at the heart of the church's mission, rather than the gospel of salvation for those who do not yet believe in Christ.

(5) There is the privatization heresy, which gives priority to private personal experiences at the expense of the fulness of the faith, such as making a certain variety of charismatic experience the litmus test of the sanctified Christian life.

All of these different types of heresy have one thing in common— they place in jeopardy the catholicity of the faith. It is those who teach heresy—often today in the name of diversity—that promote divisiveness, factiousness, and polarization, not those who call the church and all its members to celebrate its multidimensional unity in the one body of Jesus Christ.

To judge and condemn doctrine that is contrary to the gospel and to exclude from the Christian community the ungodly whose wicked conduct is scandalous calls for structures of authority that we simply do not now possess or that are not working properly. Today we must recapitulate the experience and history of the early church in developing structures of authority to deal with matters of doctrine and discipline, orthodoxy and heresy, and we must set limits to pluralism in the Christian life. In the early church, there were the rule of faith and the canon of Scripture. The Canon and the Creed were two instruments the church used to draw a line of demarcation between herself and the world.

The Reformation demonstrated its catholicity by giving the place of preeminent priority and authority to the prophetic and apostolic witnesses to the gospel of Jesus Christ. The Reformation affirmed the dogmas of the ancient ecumenical councils and their relevance in the church's struggles against heresies, schisms, sects, and cults. Luther's Catechisms are proof that Luther built the ancient dogmas of the catholic church into the evangelical faith of the Reformation. The same thing is true of the entire *Book of Concord.* The ancient ecumenical dogmas possess greater authority than the Augsburg Confession or any of the other Reformation Confessions. In writing about the relation of the ancient symbols of the faith to the later ones, David Hollaz said: "Those Creeds which were approved with the unanimous consent of the whole Catholic Church, namely, the three ecumenical symbols, possess far greater authority than those which have received the sanction and approbation of only a few particular symbols."[13]

Dietrich Bonhoeffer said: "The concept of heresy has been lost today because there isn't any teaching authority. . . . The modern ecumenical councils are anything but councils, because the word 'heresy' has been stricken from their vocabulary."[14] Among Protestant denominations, Lutherans have been known to acknowledge traditional authority structures—the authority of Holy Scripture, the Ecumenical Creeds, and their own Confessional Writings. But like other Protestants they possess no concrete official and public locus of authority whose task is to implement the authority of the normative sources of the faith. Where does the buck stop when it comes to matters of interpretation and application? Are all opinions of equal validity?

The church must have not only normative sources; it must have authoritative offices whose primary task is to teach the whole church. We do not know where these officeholders are. They seem to be in hiding. The chain of authority breaks at its weakest link. A high doctrine of the authority of Scripture, dogma, and confession will not work when their link to the concrete life of the church and its leadership is broken.

One tragedy of the Reformation is that it lost the teaching office of the church when it lost the support of the bishops. Since then, the teaching office has been wandering all over the place, in the hands of the princes; in the hands of a synod of ordained pastors; in the hands of a seminary faculty; in the hands of divisions, commissions, and task forces; and in the hands of an assembly of clergy and laity. Where is the teaching authority? What is everybody's business becomes nobody's business.

Bonhoeffer is correct: We have lost the teaching office of the church, and we seem desperately afraid to reconstitute it where it belongs in terms of the catholic tradition.[15] Pastors, of course, exercise the same powers and responsibilities as bishops in the service of the Word and Sacraments, but they do so only in their own local congregations. The difference is jurisdictional; the ministry of bishops is not only to the local church, but also to the regional and, together with other bishops, to the universal church. We lack ecumenical consensus on whether this difference is by divine right, *ius divinum,* or by human right, *ius humanum.* We may finesse the theological dispute by saying that the difference is at least a matter of fact and exists by ecclesiastical right, *ius ecclesiasticum.* The office of bishop is an element of the catholic substance of the church's tradition. It belongs to its structure of authority alongside and in the service of canonical Scripture, creedal dogma, the preaching of the gospel, and the administration of the Sacraments. The Lutheran Reformers said: "We want to declare our willingness to keep the ecclesiastical and canonical polity, provided that the bishops stop raging against our churches."[16] It is my hope that we might rediscover the wisdom of this counsel.

We may have wonderful constitutional statements about the authority of Scripture, Creeds, and Confessions, but if we have no one minding the store, such provisions are not worth more than the paper they are printed on. The doctrinal sources of authority in the church— Scripture, Creeds, and Confessions—cannot be separated from the teaching authority of the church. When the church loses the backbone of its teaching authority, it begins to look and act more and more like a jellyfish. Lutherns worldwide are bringing back the teaching office of bishops. The recovery of an authentic episcopacy, however, is no panacea for the crisis of authority in the church. It does not provide a guarantee against false teachings and practices. Many of the great heretics were bishops and some were popes. Therefore, we need the checks and balances provided by the whole church against individual aberrations. The teaching office is not a guarantee but a ministry and, like all other ministries, may be found failing or faithful.

Lutherans have stressed orthodox faith. Catholics have stressed episcopal order. Neither orthodoxy nor episcopacy alone can deal with the crisis of authority in the church. Orthodoxy without episcopacy is blind; episcopacy without orthodoxy is empty. Put the two together, and we might have a workable model of authority in the church. That was the experience of the early church; it is the lesson we must learn again from church history under the conditions of our struggles to be a church faithful to the gospel.

CHAPTER SIX

Jesus and the Church:
An Essay on Ecclesial Hermeneutics

THE QUEST OF THE HISTORICAL JESUS has again become a major preoccupation of modern New Testament scholars. It originated as a project
of the Enlightenment and continued to be carried on throughout the
nineteenth century by the application of increasingly sophisticated
methods of historical criticism. At the beginning of the twentieth century, however, dialectical and neoorthodox theologians completely
abandoned the quest as both historically impossible and theologically
irrelevant. Furthermore, they could point to Albert Schweitzer's influential history of the movement in his monumental work *The Quest of
the Historical Jesus*[1] as a kind of irrefutable obituary to the quest, even
though Schweitzer himself believed that, though all previous scholars
had failed for one reason or another, he himself had finally established
the definitive truth about the real historical Jesus. At any rate, Paul
Tillich credited Schweitzer, along with Martin Kähler, for having
placed in question the entire Jesus-research program.

Tillich wrote: "Seen in the light of its basic intention, the attempt
of historical criticism to find the empirical truth about Jesus of
Nazareth was a failure. The historical Jesus, namely, the Jesus behind
the symbols of his reception as the Christ, not only did not appear but
receded farther and farther with every new step."[2] During the heyday of
neoorthodoxy, systematic and dogmatic theologians were not really
interested in the historical Jesus. Moreover, Rudolf Bultmann, speaking
from the standpoint of critical scholarship, offered them no good

reason why they should be interested. Bultmann stated: "We can, strictly speaking, know nothing of the personality of Jesus."[3] That is no loss, because that would be to know Jesus only *kata sarka* (according to the flesh) and not *kata pneuma* (according to the spirit) (cf. 2 Corinthians 5:16). The mood of historical skepticism was pervasive and pronounced. Emil Brunner opined, "Even the bare fact of the existence of Christ as an historical person is not assured."[4]

Just when it seemed that systematic and dogmatic theology had successfully constructed their systems on purely apostolic, kerygmatic, and confessional foundations, Ernst Käsemann called for a renewal of the quest of the historical Jesus—for theological reasons. The kerygma of the exalted Lord includes the life history of Jesus and would vanish into docetic idealism without it. It was a clear protest against his teacher, Bultmann. Others of the "Old Marburgers" (Bultmannians) answered Käsemann's call, Günther Bornkamm, Hans Conzelmann, and Ernst Fuchs. The New Quest proved to be significantly different from the Old Quest entombed by Schweitzer. It did not pretend to be primarily a historico-scientific project; it was motivated chiefly by the specific interest of faith in the gospel. As a theological program, the scholars of the new quest were not in search "of supposed historical *bruta facta* but only . . . of the connection and tension between the preaching of Jesus and that of his community."[5]

Basically, the New Questers had no new methods or new texts that could solve the problem of the historical Jesus. They sought to anchor the kerygma of the church in the preaching, teaching, and activity of Jesus. Christian faith required it, otherwise it would dissolve into a kind of myth of a mystery religion. Gerhard Ebeling went on to write a comprehensive dogmatics on the basis of the theological perspective and historical findings of the new quest. Wolfhart Pannenberg agreed with the basic theological judgment of Käsemann and company that any attempt to construct Christology without going back behind the apostolic kerygma to the historical Jesus is self-contradictory, because the central christological confession of the earliest Christian community is grounded in the activity and destiny of the man Jesus. Christology is the church's interpretation of Jesus of Nazareth, his life, ministry, death, and resurrection. Pannenberg's turn to history and the historical approach constituted his decisive break with the prevailing Barthian and Bultmannian alternatives.

In this chapter I am revisiting an old theme for me. After I passed my doctoral field examinations at Harvard University in 1957, I made an appointment to see Tillich. For two years I had been wrangling with him on the Trinity and Christology, and he knew how critical I was of some of his characteristic ideas. On the issue of the place of the historical Jesus in Christology, however, I agreed with Tillich that faith and theology cannot rest on the life of the historical Jesus reconstructed by the use of the historical-critical method; they do rest on the biblical picture of Jesus as the Christ portrayed by the evangelists and apostles. When I met with Tillich, I asked him, "Now that I have passed my exams, what should I write on?" He answered, "It's clear to me. You should write on Martin Kähler, in particular his idea of 'the so-called historical Jesus and the historic biblical Christ,'" which happens to be verbatim the title of a little book Kähler published attacking the whole sweep of modern critical scholarship that set out to discover the real Jesus of history in contrast to the kerygmatic Christ of the church.[6] Nothing in English had been written on him, and the Germans had not yet begun to assess the significance of Kähler's thought for subsequent theological developments. It was Kähler who first drew a distinction in theology between *Historie* and *Geschichte,* and adopted the Greek word kerygma into the German language. In my dissertation on Kähler, I interpreted his thinking, not only against the theological background of the nineteenth century, but also in relation to his influence on Bultmann, Karl Barth, and Tillich. I also concluded that Kähler's indictments against the "life of Jesus" movement of his own day would apply in large degree to the highly reductionistic portrayals of Jesus among the scholars of the New Quest. The historical Jesus of the post-Bultmannians does not look much like the "whole Christ of the whole Bible," to use Kähler's expression. Despite the theological motivation of the New Questers, their project was still very much a continuation of the Enlightenment project, now framed by an existentialist hermeneutics.

The images of Jesus in the New Quest looked less Jewish than German, speaking Heideggerian existentialese. In line with post-World

War II West European consciousness, Jesus was portrayed as an utterly unique individual, thereby taking his historicity seriously. The task of scholarship is to focus on his will, his activity, his self-understanding, his intentionality, and his way with others. The terms ring with familiarity to anyone who read the books and articles of the New Quest. Jesus' call for decision, exemplified in his own willingness to take a risk that climaxed in his death on the cross, became the core meaning of Easter. Jesus' continuation as a person after Easter was a function of the disciples' memories of their concrete experiences of Jesus before Easter. When Pannenberg raised the question, "Well, then, did Jesus really rise from the dead?" the New Questers professed not even to understand the question. They had fumbled the ball. Willi Marxsen was most bold among the post-Bultmannian New Questers to assert that the resurrection of Jesus means the continuation of his cause after his death. The resurrection becomes a predicate of the faith of Jesus' disciples, essentially a way of seeing, rather than an event that happened to Jesus in the transition from the finality of death to a new form of eschatological life.

The New Quest is now a thing of the past. It failed both as an enterprise of critical historical scholarship and as theological exegesis of the New Testament. Now it is as dead as Bultmannian existentialist hermeneutics with its individualistic *Fragestellung* and neo-Protestant *Vorverständnis*, but now, at the end of this century, a Third Quest is under way. Its headquarters are no longer in Germany but in the English-speaking realm of theology. All three Quests have failed for the same fundamental reason. They have fallen into a chasm that separates Jesus from the church. Their approach to the historical Jesus suspends the living reality of the church as the necessary condition of affirming the essential identity of the earthly Jesus and the risen Christ. The quest of the historical Jesus, new and old, proceeds on the assumption that Jesus is dead, a passive subject of historical investigation best conducted by bracketing out the faith of his followers and their experience of his bodily presence in their eucharistic fellowship. The treatment of the resurrection in the Jesus research of today is a telltale sign that the Enlightenment and not the faith of the church is in charge of the enterprise. Enlightenment presuppositions are decisively in command. "The Enlightenment," says Francis Schüssler Fiorenza, "rejected the claim of a special divine intervention or a supernatural revelation. It therefore denied the reality of miracles and especially the miracle of the resurrection of Jesus."[7]

Apart from the resurrection as a real event in the experience of the person of Jesus, there can be no Christology and thereby no way to bridge the gap between Jesus and his church. Christology and ecclesiology play no part in the Jesus books that claim to be written on the basis of strictly historical-scientific methods. While I believe that faith has a vital interest in the historical Jesus, I affirm Kähler's point that the historical-critical method in the hands of faithless reason will produce only a "so-called historical Jesus," a product more of ideology than critical scholarship and, consequently, of negative value to Christian faith and theology. Kähler did not reject the use of the historical-critical method in biblical studies, nor do I. Historical-critical inquiry into the Gospel texts underscores the fact that Jesus of Nazareth was a real person of history, but the method by itself cannot unveil the secret of his identity apart from belief in him as the Christ of God. Much hinges on the question whether the resurrection is fact, fable, history, or myth. The rejection of the resurrection as historically real and true results in a separation between Jesus and Christ, between the fact of Jesus and his christological meaning. The legacy of Kantian epistemological dualism, the disjunction of fact and value, still underlies the scholars of the Third Quest.

The Third Quest of the Historical Jesus

In spite of historical skepticism the search for the real Jesus of history goes on. N. T. Wright refers to the current movement beyond the New Quest as the Third Quest.[8] I will adopt the term for the sake of convenience, but in the next section I will argue that from a theological point of view the Third Quest, like the Old and the New Quests, fails to take the resurrection of Jesus seriously as the necessary link to his own future as the risen Lord. Its concept of history is captive to historical positivism. What is sought is mere *Historie* and not *Geschichte*, dead history and not living history. Living history includes the horizon of the future. The real Jesus of history cannot be known in his fullness apart from the church and faith. Otherwise the Christ is separated from Jesus and lacks historical grounding, thereby becoming an arbitrary postulate of faith in a Kantian sense.

The first striking resemblance between the Third Quest and the Old Quest is the sheer fantastic variety of images of Jesus, all claiming to be based on documentary evidence and all soberly sketched by using the most scientific methods of historical-critical scholarship. Of course, the plurality of images is nothing new. Jaroslav Pelikan in his book *Jesus Through the Centuries*[9] depicts the many faces of Jesus down through the centuries. In the setting of first-century Judaism, Jesus was seen as the eschatological Messiah; to the philosophical mind-set of Hellenism, Jesus was the Logos, the rational principle of the universe. In Byzantine culture, Jesus was the perfect icon of God. In medieval times, Jesus was the monk modeling monastic discipline and self-denial. In mystical spirituality, Jesus is the bridegroom of the soul. In the Reformation tradition, Jesus is the Word of God whom the Spirit conveys in the living voice of the gospel, *viva vox evangelii*. In liberal Protestantism, Jesus is the perfect example of a socially enlightened morality. Schweitzer wrote an appropriate epitaph for how each age and each historian projected his or her own genius into his or her portrayals of Jesus:

> Each successive epoch of theology found its own thoughts in Jesus; that was, indeed, the only way in which it could make him live. But it was not only each epoch that found its reflection in Jesus; each individual created him in accordance with his own character. There is no historical task which so reveals a man's true self as the writing of a life of Jesus."[10]

Schweitzer's words apply, not only to the kaleidoscopic plurality of images in the history of Christianity and to the modern "Lives of Jesus" of the Old Quest, but also to our twentieth-century interpretations of Jesus.

"Which Jesus? Whose Jesus?" The modern quest of the historical Jesus began with a declaration of hostility to the church, its preaching about Jesus, its worship of him as the Son of God, and its dogma of the incarnation. Hans Conzelmann wrote in his article on Jesus Christ in the German theological encyclopedia *Die Religion in Geschichte und*

Gegenwart: "The historical and substantive presupposition for modern research into the life of Jesus is emancipation from traditional christological dogma on the basis of the principle of reason."[11] He was reiterating Schweitzer's judgment:

> When at Chalcedon the West overcame the East, its doctrine of the two natures dissolved the unity of the Person, and thereby cut off the last possibility of a return to the historical Jesus. . . . This dogma had first to be shattered before men could once more go out in quest of the historical Jesus, before they could grasp the thought of his existence.[12]

The religious and theological motive was to build a new Christianity, or perhaps even a new religion, on a historical Jesus freed from the church and its confession of Jesus as risen Lord. The quest of the historical Jesus, old and new, aims to ascertain what can be discovered about Jesus in isolation from his community of believers, purely as the object of methodical, critical, and historical research. The task is made difficult by the fact that Jesus appears to us exclusively through the medium of the church's memory and proclamation. The church's interest of faith was involved from the start in remembering, shaping, transmitting, gathering, and writing down all the words and events from Jesus' life, from both before and after his death on the cross.

The resurrection of Jesus stands as the driving force behind the whole process that gave rise to the New Testament. The recollections of the historical Jesus were preserved and passed on within the framework of the church's proclamation of Jesus as the risen Lord. All the Gospels are witnesses of the early church.

The Third Quest of the historical Jesus is very much like the Old Quest in that it aims to find the kernel of truth about Jesus, his very words, et cetera, inside the shell of the apostolic witness. The process of separating out the authentic words of Jesus from the later constructions of the church inevitably calls for making scholarly judgments on the basis of certain presuppositions. There is no such thing as presuppositionless research. The answers to the questions, Which Jesus? Whose Jesus? cannot be given without coming clean on the matter of presuppositions. There were certain presuppositions at work in the formation of the gospel tradition in the life of the early church. Easter and Pentecost were the crucial ones. We know what we know about Jesus only in the light of Easter and Pentecost. If we invalidate them or neutralize them as presuppositions in our approach to the historical Jesus, we will end up with a Jesus who looks very different from the Jesus Christ of the Bible and of the Christian tradition.

Schweitzer was correct in saying, "The dogma had to be shattered before men could once more go out in quest of the historical Jesus." That is to say, everything that belongs to the church's faith and doctrine, life and history, must be removed to carry on the quest of the historical Jesus. This seems to be the common methodological rule of those who search for the real Jesus of history in a purely historical-critical fashion.

The results of this Third Quest are not reassuring. For S. G. F. Brandon, Jesus was a political revolutionary; for Hugh Schonfield, a messianic schemer; for Morton Smith, the founder of a secret society; for C. F. Potter, a Qumran Essene; for Geza Vermes, a Galilean holy man; for Burton Mack, a wandering Cynic preacher; for John Dominic Crossan, a Mediterranean Jewish peasant; for Marcus Borg, a countercultural charismatic seeking the transformation of his social world, and who fits right in with the new age spirituality of today; for Elisabeth Schüssler Fiorenza, a feminist who called and formed his disciples into an egalitarian community of equals; for Barbara Thiering, a member of the Qumran community who married Mary Magdalene, had two sons and a daughter, divorced Mary and married another woman, and died some time in his sixties; for A. N. Wilson, a Galilean holy man who taught a simplified form of Judaism, without its moralism and sectarianism; for Bishop John Spong, Jesus was born of a woman who had been raped, and all the stuff about Christmas and Easter in the Gospels is nothing but the product of later Christian midrash and mythological speculation.[13] So again I ask: Which Jesus? Whose Jesus? Will the real Jesus please stand up?

More celebrated than any of these individual monographs is the group publication of scholars who formed the American "Jesus Seminar," organized by Robert Funk of the Westar Institute. These scholars discussed the sayings of Jesus and voted with colored beads—red, pink, gray, and black—to determine their relative degree of certainty. Red meant Jesus really said it. Pink meant Jesus said something nearly like it. Gray meant Jesus didn't say it but it expresses his ideas. Black meant Jesus didn't say it and the saying is placed in the mouth of Jesus from a later time. Thus the historical Jesus arises out of the obscurity of the canonical Gospels into the multicolored light of scholarly reconstructions and probability judgments. As one pundit put it, "They ran out of red ink."

A Theological Critique
of the Historical Jesus Project

Jesus is, indeed, "the Man who belongs to the world."[14] As a world-historical figure the person of Jesus, together with his influence and reputation, cannot and will not be confined to Christianity. Those who are not believing Christians and members of Christ's church will see Jesus through their own spectacles, not respecting the kerygma, liturgy, and dogma of the church. Jews, Muslims, Buddhists, and Hindus will interpret the story of Jesus in light of their own beliefs about God, humanity, religion, and morality. It is also to be expected that the academy of religious studies and biblical scholarship will do what it wants with Jesus, publishing their historical reconstructions of Jesus at whatever rate the market will bear. At the same time, it is understandable that many believing Christians will respond to the plethora of exotic constructions and novelistic fantasies about the historical Jesus much like Mary Magdalene lamented to the two angels at the tomb, "They have taken away my Lord, and I do not know where they have laid him (John 20:13)."

On his way to a village in Caesarea Philippi, Jesus asked his disciples, "Who do men say that I am (Mark 8:27)?" He followed that question with a second, "But who do you say that I am (Mark 8:29)?" He did not expect the same answer to the two questions. He expected his disciples to know better than the people in general. When Peter shot back, "You are the Christ," Jesus told them to keep it a secret (Mark 8:29-30). This exchange raises the question whether the historical-critical method, apart from any confessional submission to Jesus as the Christ within the communion of the church's experience, can best reveal the secret of the true identity and meaning of Jesus for today.

Though the Bible is the book of the church, and would not exist in its two-part canon of Testaments without the church, it has become, at the same time, an open book that belongs to all humanity. It is a book of history—the history of Israel, the history of Jesus, and the history of primitive Christianity—that can be investigated by historians around the world, religious, nonreligious, Christian, and non-Christian scholars. They all bring their own perspectives to the question: what can we know about Jesus? But how can we really know which of the pictures of Jesus that hang in the galleries of modern culture and religion is objectively true—beyond subjectivism and relativism? The historical-critical method is commonly regarded as the only adequate approach, using all the available sources and tools of modern critical scholarship. The sources and methods are public; they are not the private domain of the church. For Christian faith, this is as it should be, following as a direct implicate of taking seriously the full humanity of Jesus.

Does the historical-critical method suffice of itself? *The Christian Century* printed an exchange between John J. Collins, professor of Hebrew Bible at the University of Chicago, and Jon D. Levinson, a Jewish biblical scholar at Harvard Divinity School, on the competence of historical criticism in biblical interpretation.[15] John Collins reviewed together Brevard S. Childs's *Biblical Theology of the Old and New Testaments*[16] and Levinson's *The Hebrew Bible, The Old Testament and Historical Criticism: Jews and Christians in Biblical Studies.*[17] He criticized both scholars for the same reason: they combine confessional faith with historical criticism. Collins writes, "Biblical Scholars . . . regard a theological interest as at best irrelevant and at worst a distorting influence."[18] He goes on to say that the postulate of divine revelation on which faith and theology depend is irrelevant to historical criticism and can "only lead to obscurantism by cutting off the quest for a naturalistic, human explanation."[19] He adds, "A tendency toward historical distortion is inevitably present when one attempts to combine historical criticism with theological orthodoxy."[20] Collins finds Childs guilty of Barthian Protestantism and Levinson of Orthodox

Judaism. The alleged result is compromise. The confessional approach of Childs and Levinson, a Christian and a Jew, privileges certain theological commitments. "They are willing to participate fully in the historical-critical conversation so long as theological issues are not at stake."[21] Of Levinson's performance Collins writes: "His dalliance with historical criticism ends in *coitus interruptus,* since he pulls back before the final consummation."[22]

Levinson answers Collins in a subsequent issue of *The Christian Century.*[23] Collins's position, says Levinson, claims for historical criticism an exclusive and absolute access to the truth about the Bible, naively assuming that the principles underlying historical criticism are intrinsic to universal human reason and lie above and beyond the limits of historical relativity and cultural particularity.[24]

Levinson deals directly with the issue of historical criticism and the Bible in an article entitled, "The Bible: Unexamined Commitments of Criticism," which appeared in *First Things.*[25] The point he makes is that historical critics belong to a community of interpretation with its own prior assumptions—secular analogues to the religious commitments Jews and Christians bring to the texts of the Bible. Those who think that the historical-critical method is value neutral are self-deceived.

Ernst Troeltsch spelled out the fundamental principles of the historical-critical method: (1) the critical principle of methodological doubt; (2) the principle of analogy that says that all events are similar in principle; (3) the principle of correlation, the notion that all phenomena are interrelated and interdependent, subject to relations of cause and effect. Collins adds a fourth, the principle of autonomy, which means that neither church nor state can prescribe in advance what scholars must prove.

Collins thinks, says Levinson, that the commonly accepted "axioms of Troeltschian historicism are not 'prior commitments.'"[26] Collins ignores the social character of knowledge. Historical critics operate with a set of assumptions that are no more self-evident and free of cultural particularism than the confessional commitments of Jews and Christians. Why should the church be asked to surrender its "prior commitments" anymore than the academy? Historical critics assume that they enjoy the privileged position of pursuing the truth wherever it may lead, without regard to any outside collectivity, religious or political, but, in that, they are fooling themselves. Levinson observes, "The academy has its own equivalents of excommunication and the revocation of membership."[27] Christian scholars should not be intimidated. Their commitments of faith have been condemned as irrelevant, obscurantist, or distortive by the positivistic historicists. It's time for them to challenge their secular colleagues to acknowledge the prior assumptions of their own community of interpretation and to admit that they lack grounds to be making their supposedly value-neutral totalistic claims.[28]

The upshot of this exchange is that the historical-critical method does not exist as a naked and neutral set of research operations. It cannot, through historical reconstruction, build a bridge to our contemporary situation. A hermeneutical factor must come into play.

"Which hermeneutic? Whose hermeneutic?" The hermeneutic of the autonomous scholar who keeps his or her own confessional commitment private and hidden behind a cloak of positivistic historicism, or that of a community of faithful memory that forthrightly acknowledges the biblical writings as canonical? The fact of canon means that inquiry into the biblical texts—in this case, the quest of the historical Jesus—cannot be detached from the community that produced them and has kept them alive in an ongoing process of interpretation. In other words, if a hermeneutical factor is unavoidably entailed in every application of the historical-critical method, then it would seem reasonable to honor the tradition of interpretation of the religious community for whom the Bible is more than a haphazard collection of ancient writings. Levinson warns biblical scholars of the folly of "sawing off the branch on which they are sitting."[29]

I am suggesting that the church is intrinsic to a hermeneutic of historical inquiry in search of the true identity and meaning of Jesus of Nazareth. This is clearly implied in Childs's "canonical method" of biblical interpretation, a method that Levinson endorses as equally applicable to the Jewish approach to the Hebrew Bible.

The hermeneutical significance of the church in answering the question, "Who was Jesus of Nazareth?" is also very evident in the writings of Wright, until recently a New Testament theologian at Worcester

College, Oxford. In the Preface of his book *Who Was Jesus?* Wright asserts: "Among other beliefs, I hold more firmly than ever to the conviction that serious study of Jesus and the Gospels is best done within the context of a worshipping community."[30] An ecclesially oriented hermeneutic cannot produce facts that do not exist, nor can it use the historical-critical method merely to rubber stamp a belief system that existed prior to historical inquiry. It does enter into the formation of scholarly judgments and decisions about matters of fact and interpretation. I am not so sanguine as Wright about the theological promise of what he calls the Third Quest, referring to the books about Jesus written by Vermes, Brandon, E. P. Sanders, Borg, and others, but I do think that he is pushing Jesus research in a theological direction that overcomes G. E. Lessing's "ugly ditch" between historical facts and eternal truth, reflected in the split between history and faith.

Although Wright prefers the Third Quest to the Old and the New, he finds that it, too, is impaled on the separation of history and theology. Serious historical study of Jesus is the starting point for serious theological study, that is, the beginning of Christology and the foundation of the church. He rightly faults the Third Quest for having nothing to say about Easter and, thereby, failing to find the bridge connecting Jesus and the church. He says, "Serious historical research cannot remain silent here of all places."[31] Here the historical question is, at the same time, a matter of immediate theological concern. Wright says, "The central Christian claim is that Jesus of Nazareth was raised from the dead three days after his execution. I have argued . . . that as historians we are forced to take this claim very seriously indeed. The alternative explanations, when examined, turn out to be remarkably lame."[32]

Why do the historical critics ignore or explain away what happened at Easter? Wright is correct in writing: "There is a hole in the historical jigsaw-puzzle at just this point. One major test of any hypothesis about the history of the first century is how well it can cope with this hole."[33] Wright exposes the common opinion in almost all modern Jesus studies, the assumption that because the resurrection is indeed a matter of faith, it cannot at the same time be a historical event. This assumption functions as a virtual dogma among historical critics and is subscribed to even by many who claim to be Christian. "The Gospels (we are told) are faith-documents; therefore, they are not about history."[34] If something can be explained as belonging to the faith of the primitive Christian community, it must be subtracted from the Jesus side of the ledger. This won't work, though, because Jesus himself, his very being as the person he was, brings history and faith into the same focus. What we have in the New Testament is "theological history."[35] What the Gospels narrate is not the story of the "historical Jesus" who lurks like a ghost behind the texts to be reincarnated by modern critical historiography, but the canonical biblical Christ who is identical with the earthly Jesus. Immanuel Kant's epistemological dualism continues to cast its shadow on the commonly accepted divorce between facts and meanings in contemporary biblical scholarship.

Elements of Ecclesial Hermeneutics

Theological-historical exegesis is a function of the worshiping church. Outside the framework of the church, scholars will look for traces of a dead Jesus in first-century Palestine. Rabbi Peter Levinson of Heidelberg was quoted in *Time* magazine as saying: "If I believed in Jesus' resurrection, I would be baptized tomorrow."[36] Would that make a difference in what and how a scholar would write about Jesus? For example, Geza Vermes, a Jewish scholar, writes about Jesus in a way that can be fully accounted for within the limits of Judaism alone.[37] He concludes from his research that the church's confessions concerning Jesus Christ "have little to do with the religion preached and practiced by him."[38] It was the Christ of Paul and John who

> overshadows and obscures the man of Galilee. . . . Jesus' eyes were fixed on God and his Kingdom. Those of his followers, in particular Paul, focused on the risen and glorified Lord. The purely theocentric religion of Jesus became a christocentric faith in which the heavenly Father plays practically no role. . . . Is it an exaggeration to suggest that oceans separate Paul's Christian Gospel from the religion of Jesus the Jew?[39]

It is the appearance of Jesus of Nazareth as the risen Lord that distinguishes the perspective of Paul, a first-century Jew, from that of

Vermes, a twentieth-century Jew. Paul and John, worse than Judas, are
the ones who really betrayed Jesus. "John's Christ," says Vermes, "has
nothing in common with the real Jesus."[40] Vermes sees sheer disconti-
nuity. John saw and expressed continuity between the earthly Jesus and
the risen Christ in these words: "But the Counselor, the Holy Spirit,
whom the Father will send in my name, he will teach you all things,
and bring to your remembrance all that I have said to you (John
14:26)." Appeal to the Spirit was also expressed by Paul:

> So also no one comprehends the thoughts of God except the Spirit
> of God. Now we have received not the spirit of the world, but the
> Spirit which is from God, that we might understand the gifts
> bestowed on us by God. And we impart this in words not taught by
> human wisdom but taught by the Spirit, interpreting spiritual
> truths to those who possess the Spirit (1 Cor. 2:11-13).

If Christian scholars bracket out the Holy Spirit, alive and at work
in the church—the community in which Christ is sacramentally present in his body and blood (the *totus Christus, caput et corpus*)—their
historical-critical treatments of the Gospel narratives will probably
become hermeneutically incoherent. Only the witness of the Spirit
through the apostles can disclose the meaning of Jesus' life and death.
Without the Spirit, the historian, at best, would find only an empty
grave on Easter but no risen Savior. The outcome of a Spiritless
hermeneutic of Scripture is to interpret the life of Jesus in categories
inappropriate to him. This phenomenon accounts, in large part, for the
bewildering variety of modern images of Jesus—Jesus is a holy man,
Jesus is a revolutionary, Jesus is a feminist, Jesus is gay, Jesus is black,
Jesus is a mushroom eater, and Jesus is a cross between a Gnostic and a
Cynic, and so on. Such interpretations of the historical Jesus are guided
by extracanonical paradigms dictated by the elemental spirits of the
age, *stoicheia,* and not the Holy Spirit of God and the Lord Jesus
Christ.

Walter Kasper emphasizes the activity of the Spirit in overcoming
the gulf between Jesus and the church. In an article, "The Church as
Sacrament of the Spirit,"[41] Kasper corrects a one-sidedness found in the
post-Bultmannian hermeneutics of Fuchs and Ebeling that places the

quest of the historical Jesus exclusively within the framework of "Word and Faith" to the neglect of "Spirit and Church." The Eastern Orthodox emphasis on pneumatology in constructing both Christology and ecclesiology offers a useful balance to the predominantly if not exclusively christological foundation of ecclesiology in both Protestant and Roman Catholic forms of Western theology. It is only the experience of Jesus as the Christ in the power of the Spirit that founded and perpetuated the church after Jesus' death and resurrection.

Faith, too, is an essential link in the hermeneutical chain that connects Jesus and the church. *Fides quaerens intellectum!* Also, with respect to the study of Jesus, faith is an element in the process of coming to knowledge. Philip Melanchthon coined the formula: "To know Christ is to know his benefits." Genuine Christian knowledge presupposes a living faith in the salvific presence of God incarnate in Jesus Christ. It is an immediate analytic judgment of faith that the person of Jesus is in some way homogeneous with the self-revealing God of Israel. The trinitarian and christological dogmas of the church express this truth in highly sophisticated ontological categories. An ecclesial hermeneutic will judge these dogmas as true interpretation of the historical Jesus who is at the same time the kerygmatic Christ.

Church history illustrates that the abandonment of this orthodox ecclesial perspective leads either to Judaizing christological tendencies on the left, *ebionitism,* or to gnosticizing tendencies on the right, *docetism.* Either Jesus was nothing but a mere man, or he was a supernatural ghost and not even human. The witness of the Holy Spirit, the *testimonium spiritus sancti internum,* creates the knowledge of faith concerning the true identity and meaning of Jesus Christ. In contrast, the historical Jesus reconstructed by critical scholarship never becomes more than a matter of higher or lower degrees of probability. Nothing is certain, so there can be no basis for the assurance of faith. A merely probable historical Jesus can never become the living Christ of faith. The Holy Spirit bridges faith and Christ by raising the historical Jesus out of the remoteness of past history into the context of contemporary ecclesial experience as the living Christ.

The living Christ becomes really present by the witness of the Holy Spirit in the experience of faith through the church's preaching of the Word. The evangelical reformation emphasis on Word and Faith, however reductionistically it was developed in modern Protestantism, must be embraced in a more comprehensive catholic and orthodox hermeneutics of Spirit and Church. The work of the Holy Spirit is not to blow his own horn, but to serve as the inner dynamism of the living voice of the gospel of Christ, *viva vox evangelii*. The Spirit is not a function of an individual's personal religious experience; he is rather the power of the preaching of Jesus as the Christ. Otherwise, the words of preaching are only dead wires with no current running through them!

Apart from the Spirit and the church, there is no knowledge of the historical Jesus that has the power to awaken faith. Cyprian's formula is exactly right: *extra ecclesiam nulla salus!* It seems somewhat odd that a Lutheran should be saying this when many Roman Catholic scholars seem to have abandoned it out of embarrassment. Apart from the church, there is no communication concerning Jesus that can lead to a confession of him as Savior and Lord. The profane quest of the historical Jesus is not only powerless to awaken faith, but may actually pose an obstacle in the way of grasping what is essential in the New Testament picture of Jesus of Nazareth.

The church is a sacrament and instrument of the Holy Spirit. The Holy Spirit not only works through the church, but the church is his dwelling place. Therefore, the church is the realm within which the true identity and meaning of Jesus can be known and confessed.

The canonical method of biblical interpretation, to which I referred in the exchange between Levinson and Collins, is usually associated with the name of Childs. Childs would not claim, however, that he invented the method. In its fundamental elements, it has been the classical approach practiced within the liturgical and dogmatic life of the church. The whole Christ of the whole Bible, and not some historical Jesus behind the scriptural texts, is the object of inquiry of the canonical method applied for the sake of the total life and worship of the church.

The biblical texts in their final shape, just as they are, convey a trustworthy picture of Jesus as the one whom his apostles confessed as Lord and Savior. The simple Christian has access to this picture in the same way as a biblical scholar, even though he or she is unable to decompose the picture into the original elements that went into its making. It is the picture of the whole biblical Christ that has impressed itself on the memory of his community in the light of the Holy Spirit. The modern scholarly reconstructions of the historical Jesus are theologically suspect because they are used as substitutes for the apostolic picture of Jesus; they claim to set the record straight, to give us, at last, the historical truth about the real Jesus of Nazareth, which is a different Jesus than the person we meet in the apostolic preaching of Jesus as the Christ.

The Interpretation of the Bible in the Church

We have come to the end of our reflection on the relevance of ecclesial hermeneutics for the quest of the historical Jesus. Our theological critique of the quest, in all its manifestations, is offered in light of an approach which we have variously referred to as ecclesial hermeneutics, theological exegesis, or the canonical method. This approach finally hinges on the issue of the authority of the Bible as the word of God. The authority of Scripture lies at the heart of our concept of ecclesial hermeneutics. The uniqueness and authority of Scripture are meaningless concepts to biblical critics for whom early Christianity is just one of several Hellenistic propaganda religions or for whom the biblical writings can be interpreted exhaustively within the arena of human experience and human reason.

The Pontifical Biblical Commission has issued a document entitled *The Interpretation of the Bible in the Church*.[42] This document provides a strong affirmation of the historical-critical method of exegesis; yet, it warns exegetes of the dangers of ignoring the believing community as the truly adequate context for interpreting the canonical Scriptures. In this context, faith, the Holy Spirit, and church authority are necessary to remain faithful to the great tradition that produced the canon. The canonical writings, says the document, possess "a salvific and theological value completely different from that attaching to other ancient texts."[43] It recognizes "the fact that the Holy Spirit is the principal author of the Bible," and that the light of the Spirit and faith lived in ecclesial community are needed to be faithful to the revelation of

God attested by the Bible. These are the perennial presuppositions of a hermeneutics that deliberately places itself within the living tradition of the church. If biblical scholars do not proceed from such an ecclesial preunderstanding in their historical and exegetical work, they have the burden of proving that any alternative set of presuppositions is better suited for the task of biblical interpretation. The church has a long record of experience in reading, rereading, and recontextualizing the Scriptures; it will not be easily convinced that it has missed the mark from the moment it began to translate its memories into manuscript and pass them along through the subsequent centuries of biblical inter-pretation.

CHAPTER SEVEN

Doing Theology for the Church under the Authority of Scripture

THE FIRST LINE of Paul Tillich's *Systematic Theology* reads: "Theology, as a function of the Christian church, must serve the needs of the church."[1] Perhaps theologians are in danger of forgetting that when theology is increasingly treated as a therapeutic exercise in reflecting on one's personal religious experience. Today, we encounter everywhere the triumph of the category of experience in theology. The neoorthodox critique of Friedrich Schleiermacher's experiential method has been overturned by the rebirth of neoliberal theology. As with Schleiermacher, only those contents of the Christian faith that emanate from one's own religious experience and conform to today's culture-religion are acceptable. The rest is jettisoned.

Experience, of course, is important and necessary. I agree with Tillich's statement: "Experience is the medium through which the sources 'speak' to us. . . . Experience is not the source from which the contents of systematic theology are taken but the medium through which they are existentially received."[2] Tillich's judgment in the 1950s is equally valid today. He wrote: "The encounter with great non-Christian religions, the evolutionary scheme of thought, the openness for the new which characterizes the pragmatic method, have had the consequence that experience has become not only the main source of systematic theology but an inexhaustible source out of which new truths can be taken continually. Being open for new experiences which might even pass beyond the confines of Christian experience is now the proper attitude of the theologian. He is not bound to a circle the center of which is the event of Jesus as the Christ."[3] Then Tillich says: "Christian theology is based on the unique event Jesus the Christ, and in spite of the infinite meaning of this event it remains this event and, as such, the criterion of every religious experience. This event is given to experience and not derived from it. Therefore, experience receives and does not produce. . . . The systematic theologian is bound to the Christian message which he must derive from other sources than his experience under the criterion of the norm."[4] For Tillich, that norm is "the new Being in Jesus as the Christ as our ultimate concern."[5]

Theology today is running riot in pluralism. The major cause of radical pluralism in theology is that theology has become an account of the varieties of experience, social, cultural, linguistic, and religious. According to traditional theology, God decided to create man in his own image. Then Ludwig Feuerbach said, in effect, "It's time to return the compliment." If experience becomes the source of theology, we can reimagine God in all sorts of ways. That is the root of radical pluralism. "A divine being," wrote Tillich, "in the traditional sense is excluded from such a theology."[6]

Doing theology, under the authority of Scripture within the context of the church, is an alternative to theology as "experiential expressivism," to use the term coined by George Lindbeck.[7] If we are clear about the sources and norms of theology, it should be possible to do theology in an ecumenical age on a collaborative model. Whatever our confessional background, we should teach the one apostolic faith of the holy catholic church, and not merely the particular doctrines of a modern sect. I would not deny that my religious experience and confessional context color the interpretation I give to the matter, but it is precisely for that reason that an ecumenical collaborative model is important to set limits to the pluralism arising from the subjective idiosyncrasies of each theologian. There is, of course, no universal dogmatics, one for all times and places.

Not so long ago, it was thought that dogmatics was dead or dying. Ernst Troeltsch wrote seventy-five years ago: "Dogmatics is a discipline which exists today only in the narrowest of theological circles, and even there it languishes." Immediately thereafter, Karl Barth renewed dogmatics as a discipline of the church. Instead of dying, it has actually flourished in the twentieth century. In recent years we have witnessed an outpouring of new publications from different confessional traditions—Roman Catholic, Anglican, Lutheran, Reformed, Methodist, Baptist, Mennonite, and others. The best examples do not practice the experiential method to create new theology for a new Christianity. Barth's legacy endures in that these works of theology claim to be faithful to what believers in Christ and members of his church believe on the basis of God's special revelation in Jesus Christ. That is the center that holds all things together in an ecumenically oriented dogmatics.

Vincent, the fifth-century monk of Lerins, became famous for saying: "In the Catholic Church all possible care should be taken that we hold that faith which has been believed everywhere, always and by all." (*Quod ubique, quod semper, quod ab omnibus*). The center of that faith, the one thing that all Christians and all churches in all times and places share, is the gospel of Jesus Christ according to the Scriptures.

One of the earliest summaries of the gospel comes from the apostle Paul in 1 Cor. 15:3-6.

> For I delivered to you as of first importance what I also received, that Christ died for our sins in accordance with the scriptures, that he was buried, that he was raised on the third day in accordance with the scriptures, and that he appeared to Cephas, then to the twelve.

The revelation in Jesus Christ is the gospel of God. Some theologians from different schools are clamoring for theocentricity (for example, John Hick, Paul Knitter, W. C. Smith, James Gustafson, Rosemary Radford Ruether, and Tom Driver), and they propose to achieve this at the expense of Christology. This is a false move; it contradicts the ecumenical center of the faith—the revelation of God in Jesus Christ. The gospel that Jesus preached (Mk. 1:14) and the gospel Paul preached about Jesus (Rom. 1:1 and 2 Cor. 11:7) are nothing other than the gospel of God which was a long time in preparation, going back to the dawn of history and the election of Israel. When we unpack the phrase "the gospel of Jesus Christ," we are not affirming a Christomonism that separates Jesus from God's covenant people through whom he gave the law and the promise as a *praeparatio evangelica*. The God who speaks in his

Son Jesus is the same God who spoke of old through the prophets (Heb. 1:1). Jesus as Messiah turned out to be the content of the prophetic message that God delivered to Israel before Jesus was born, as the apostles told the story.

To affirm that God revealed himself uniquely in Jesus Christ does not deny that God has communicated to all people something of his "eternal power and deity . . . in the things that have been made" (Rom. 1:20). In a sense that must be carefully defined, there is a universal revelation of God that can be known apart from God's covenant with Israel. This, of course, has been a controversial point in contemporary theology and is decisive for theological method.

Two Ways of Doing Theology

Among theologians who accept the revelation of God in Jesus Christ as the decisive center of a theology faithful to the Scriptures, there are broadly two strategies that contend with each other. In his magisterial work, *God as the Mystery of the World*, Eberhard Jüngel observes that "there are two approaches in contemporary theology by which the attempt is made to learn to think God again."[8] One of the two ways is to start with anthropology, a method pursued by Wolfhart Pannenberg. From this basis, Pannenberg moves to the idea of God as the necessary frame of reference for a discussion of the Christian understanding of the Trinity based on God's revelation in Jesus Christ. Pannenberg moves from the self-transcending dimension of human experience outside the circle of Christian faith to the confession of the triune God inside the church. Jüngel's approach is the other way around. He begins his theology from within the specifically Christian circle of belief in the self-revealing God of the Bible. Pannenberg starts outside and goes inside, and Jüngel starts inside and goes outside. In principle both cover the same ground. One opens the banquet of theology with the cold soup of general anthropological foundations established by reason alone, the other serves the hot soup of the revelatory word in the exclusive medium of faith.

As Jüngel says, these are opposite approaches. Yet, both have their adherents in the history of Christian theology. The issue was crisply formulated by Tertullian: "What does Jerusalem have to do with Athens?" The Middle Ages witnessed a clash of methods between the Augustinians and the Aristotelians over the question of the knowledge of God. Tillich described it well in his essay, "The Two Types of Philosophy of Religion."[9] The question, simply put, is: Do we start theology with God as the first principle, first not only in the order of being but also in the order of knowing? Or, do we start with our experience of life here and now, and then approach the idea of God and God's revelation as we meet it in the texts and traditions of Christian faith? Do we start from above, with the word of God *tout simple*, or do we start from below, with common human experience? Tillich wrote: "The divergence between these two approaches to the knowledge of God is the great problem of the philosophy of religion."[10]

The theological approaches of Jüngel and Pannenberg are indeed very different. They start at opposite ends of the spectrum, but, surprisingly, their methodological differences do not yield a material dogmatic difference in their doctrine of the triune God and the place of Jesus in the Trinity. Neither falls into the pit of experiential subjectivism. Both approaches are oriented to the ecumenical center of Christian dogmatics, the normative status of God's revelation in Jesus Christ. Both do theology under the authority of Scripture within the context of the church. Nevertheless, there is a difference, and one must choose which way to go.

After my extended lament about the inflation of experience in contemporary theology, it may seem odd that methodologically my preference is for the way of Pannenberg (and Tillich) rather than the way of Jüngel (and Barth). In 1950, Pannenberg was a student of theology at the University of Basel. Years later, Pannenberg gave Barth a copy of his book on Christology, *Jesus—God and Man*. Later they had an exchange of letters. Barth lamented that Pannenberg was steering back to the old shores, back to the old way of thinking from below to above, from common human experience to the particularity of Christian faith. Barth ended his letter by saying: "If you will pardon the harsh expression, I can only regard your own path as reactionary."[11] At about the same time Barth also wrote to Jüngel, expressing how pleased he was with the direction of Jüngel's thinking. He wrote: "I have learned to know you as one among today's younger theologians who has studied me thoroughly and has the willingness and ability to do independently and fruitfully the further work which is needed today."[12] Jüngel today is carrying on the legacy of Barth's way—the rejection of the foundational function of philosophy in providing a prior rational justification of the idea of God on the basis of anthropology.

Is there a place for philosophy in relation to theology? Is there a place for natural theology in a theology of revelation that affirms the uniqueness of Jesus Christ? I think the answer is yes to both questions, and that answer is consistent with the mainstream of the classical Christian tradition. Philosophy can formulate the minimal conditions of an existentially meaningful and rationally justifiable talk about God in human religion. Religion is an inalienable structure of being human. Christian theology would be foolish to throw religion to the dogs of atheistic criticism.

It is not theologically wise to surrender to the atheistic accounts of religion in human experience and the modern world, from Feuerbach's theory of God-language as a projection of human longing for infinity, to Karl Marx's theory of God-language as the consolation of the poor serving the special interests of the rich, to Sigmund Freud's notion of God as an infantile illusion, and to Friedrich Nietzsche's interpretation of religion as springing from the resentment of the masses. Pannenberg defends the interest of Christian theology in attacking these negative voices on the basis of a fundamental reflection on the meaning of religion in human existence by appealing, not directly to the authority of revelation, but to evidences judged in the light of reason. It is not reasonable to say, as some theologians in the school of Albrecht Ritschl used to say, "If I were not a Christian, I would be an atheist."

God is not dead in the experience of most modern people, as the polls indicate, and that experience is not irrelevant to the Christian understanding of God's special revelation in Jesus Christ. Pannenberg takes the long road, writing chapters on the human experience of religion and the knowledge of God in the pre- and non-Christian religions before getting to the trinitarian God of biblical revelation. For Barth and Jüngel, this is to build the house of dogmatics on the quicksand of philosophical speculation and historical research. Why bother to build a ramp from human experience and knowledge in the areas of reason, history, religion, morality, society, and nature, as Pannenberg does, and not begin and end within the "holy of holies" of the Bible and the Christian gospel?

The temptation is great to chuck the entire affair of apologetics. Classical apologetics was conducted as natural theology. Today, it takes the form of foundational theology. In renouncing the apologetic task, theology can concentrate all its creative energies on biblical interpretation, church dogmatics, and liturgical language for the sake of the church. I am not opposed to the good works that result from this approach, but I think it is not the only way. Pannenberg himself never thought of his theological program in polar opposition to Barth's trinitarian theology of revelation. In 1965 Pannenberg wrote to Barth:

> I was bold enough to hope that you would perceive in my work a continuation of the basic thought of your theology of revelation in a changed intellectual climate. . . . I would like to express my conviction that . . . it will still be possible to continue your concentration of theology on the truth of the revelation of God in Jesus Christ, which transcends all our human questioning and speaking. I shall never cease to be grateful that I learned from you to focus all theological work on this center.[13]

Being clear about the dogmatic center makes it possible to explore the wider circumference without losing one's way. The purely intraecclesial and intratextual dogmatic option of Barth, Jüngel, and their antifoundationalist friends cannot monopolize the question of God and its answer. The issues of contemporary consciousness press in upon us, and they exceed the limits of the Bible and the church. A comprehensive approach to systematic theology should take responsibility for the entire waterfront of issues that concern people who already believe in Christ as well as those who do not yet believe. This is why I opt for an approach that John Macquarrie has called "a new style of natural theology,"[14] and I believe that Pannenberg has carried it out in the most brilliant fashion.

Signals of Transcendence

The question of God is a religious question, one that Christians share with people of all religions and even of no religion at all. The question of God arises out of the human quest for meaning. Religious symbols, images, and metaphors are the language that enshrine the human search for a transcendent fulfillment beyond the limits of human finitude. Through analysis of the transphenomenal dimension of human subjectivity it can be shown that humans strive beyond all the givens of their worldly experience to discover what lies beyond the boundary line drawn by the certainty of death. Peter Berger has referred to these experiential elements in the self-surpassing openness of the human subject as "signals of transcendence."[15]

Such signals are not like the proofs of the existence of God in the old-style natural theology. New-style natural theology stops short of claiming to possess definitive knowledge of God and God's will unto salvation, upon which the Christian life of faith, hope, and love is founded. It does ground the meaning of the idea of God in the structures of common human experience. It means to start theology from below, from the side of the human subject inquiring into the possibilities of meaning in existence and history. It does not begin from above, from the sheer datum of revelation.

If we look for traces of transcendence in human experience and language, we will gain some points of contact for the specifically Christian language of God coming from the Bible and the traditions of the church. There are, in fact, experiential occasions in which a rupturing of our ordinary language takes place, and we blurt out something like, "Oh, my God." These are situations of despair and hope, wonder and terror, dread and peace, and abandonment and joy. Such experiences as described by existentialist phenomenology can prove helpful to Christian theology, not in the sense of proving the reality of God or the truth of the Christian revelation, but in the sense of re-connecting our language about God with the lived experiences of people of all times. Having witnessed many philosophical fashions come and go, I am still partial to Tillich's judgment: "Existentialism is the good luck of Christian theology."[16]

It may be argued that what we have called a new-style natural theology is not theology at all. It is nothing more than a kind of philosophical anthropology. Existentialism is at best oriented to the human search for transcendence; it cannot deliver true and saving knowledge of God. It can focus on the limit situations of human existence and the symbols that express the human quest for fulfillment beyond the negativities of existence. The question for theology is whether religious language that expresses the human quest for transcendence is referential in kind, whether the word "god" that appears in the religions is only an idea or points beyond itself to reality. Is God real? Does God really exist beyond our imaginative projections? Or are we only whistling in the dark?

Philosophy may pretend it's in good shape without a positive answer to the question of God's existence, but it is fatal for theology not to answer this question in a positive way. Langdon Gilkey put his finger on the problem: "The reality of God and so of the referent of religious language is the central point at issue."[17] Real theology presupposes belief in the reality of the referent to which its language points, otherwise the religious experience it seeks to account for becomes vacuous.

The Principle of Referentiality

Currently there is under way a movement in theology which boldly surrenders the principle of referentiality. Sharon D. Welch has written a feminist theology of liberation. She begins her book *Communities of Resistance and Solidarity* with a chapter titled "The Fundamental Crisis in Christian Theology." The problem, she writes, "concerns the reality referent of Christian faith and thus of Christian theology."[18] She goes on:

> Paul, Aquinas, Luther, and Tillich all assume that faith refers to something real, an experience of ultimacy that is in some way actual and present, an ultimacy that limits and shapes the nature of theological inquiry. We modern academic theologians no longer have the surety of such a referent.[19]

Gordon Kaufman, too, teaches that God language is merely the imaginative construction of the human mind. Other theologians follow the same line of interpretation in which religious words and symbols are solely the products of human imagination and the projection of human values and wishes. The ghost of Feuerbach, no longer hiding in the background, is now leading the band of theological deconstructionists.

Philosophy, or any new-style natural theology, that conducts its analysis of "religion within the limits of reason alone" is not able to assure us that the idea of a transcendent God is more than a useful fiction. Something like Bernard Lonergan's notion of a conversion of the mind is required, involving the intellectual, moral, and religious dimensions of the whole person. This conversion of the mind is faith, an act of the whole person. The conviction that the word "God" refers to the being of God and is something more than a noise within the echo chamber of the human psyche is itself an experience that can be described and defined. Tillich calls it "ultimate concern," Rudolf Bultmann "existential commitment," and Hans Küng "basic trust." Why not simply call it "faith," along with the Bible and the Christian tradition?

Christian theology is possible only on the condition of faith, and faith is an existential relation to God. The God of Christian faith is not an abstract transcendence beyond the horizon of our finite world of history and society. As Søren Kierkegaard held, Christian faith is related to the Absolute Paradox; the Eternal has entered history at one point in time in a definitive way. The living God reveals himself under the conditions of existence and history in the person of Jesus Christ. The dogma of the incarnation is the dividing line between philosophy and theology, natural theology and biblical revelation. In plain and simple words, it is the gospel that makes the difference—the gospel of God in the personal life and history of Jesus of Nazareth.

The travesty today is that many schools of theology do not heed the dividing line, the difference. Within the last decade we have witnessed an attack on the principle of christocentricity in constructing the Christian doctrine of God. This is the case with some forms of process theology (Schubert Ogden and John Cobb), radical theological feminism (Sallie McFague, Carter Heyward, Rosemary R. Ruether, Sheila Davaney, Welch), and the pluralistic theology of religions (John

Hick, Paul Knitter, Wilfred Cantwell Smith). They are all anti-incarnational. They all deny the particularity and uniqueness of God's revelation in Jesus Christ according to the Scriptures and the Ecumenical Creeds. They deny the exclusivity claim of the apostolic kerygma—the confession that Jesus Christ is the one and only Savior of humankind. Here the God of the philosophers has eclipsed the God of our father Abraham, who is identical with the Father of our Lord Jesus Christ in the biblical history of salvation.

Martin Luther once said that the author of the Fourth Gospel was not a Platonist but an evangelist. The metaphysical assumption of the new antichristologists is Platonist, or better neo-Platonist. They have a problem with the idea of an ontological union of the infinite and the finite. It is an ancient problem. The absolute of Hellenistic metaphysics found it ontologically impossible to live and move and have its being in history, in human form, in a state of suffering and death. The God of Hellenistic metaphysics is impassable and immortable. Such a God would never be caught dead in the person of Jesus and his destiny on the cross.

What we have called a new-style natural theology functions only as prolegomenon to the specifically Christian understanding of the Trinity based on God's revelation in Jesus Christ. The God of the gospel is capable of assuming the identity, attributes, and experiences of human being in the world, and this is neither conceptually unintelligible nor ontologically impossible.

Revelation and Salvation

If human knowledge of God is based solely on revelation, the question arises whether such revelation occurs in religions other than Christian—whether it can be apprehended outside the walls of the church and beyond the pages of Scripture. To affirm with Paul and the classical Christian tradition that God has revealed something of his will and nature in other religions does not mean that they already possess, in other words and symbols, the revelation of God in Jesus Christ. What is unique about God's revelation in Jesus Christ is Jesus Christ himself. Revelation in Christ is the coming of God himself in the power and glory of his kingdom; it is the dawning of the new age in the personal life, death, and resurrection of Jesus as God's Messiah promised to Israel's prophets. There's nothing like this in any of the religions, no matter how much they might otherwise witness to truth, beauty, and goodness.

Every theology after Barth has felt obliged to establish itself as a theology of revelation. In an early reaction Paul Althaus called attention to the inflation of the concept of revelation in contemporary theology.[20] This inflation was brought about by the epistemological crisis in modern theology signaled by Kant's critiques of reason. There is good reason, however, to question the dominant role that revelation plays in modern theology. Revelation is not the supreme category of biblical theology and Christian dogmatics; God's work of salvation in history is! The supremacy of revelation assumes that the basic human predicament is the lack of the knowledge of God. From a biblical perspective, however, God is engaged in dealing with the active rebellion of the human will. Human will is in bondage to cosmic powers beyond itself. Sin and Death in capital letters come into focus. Then reconciliation—not revelation, which answers the question of knowledge— becomes the key motif as the answer to the question of sin as estrangement. Furthermore, when revelation becomes the focal point of dogmatics, it relegates Jesus Christ primarily to the role of revelation. Then, in the interest of constructing a high Christology in line with John and Paul, theology is driven to make Jesus Christ the sole revelation of God, the absolutely exclusive medium of revelation.

In biblical theology, however, God is revealed in Jesus Christ but not first and only in him. There is a twofold revelation of God, through the law of creation and through the gospel of redemption. There is the revelation, not only of God's love in Jesus Christ, but also of divine law through the structures of creation and the demands of justice. It is just as essential to draw the proper distinction between revelation and salvation as between law and gospel. Not all revelation is salvific; there is also revelation of divine wrath and judgment through world-historical events and personal experiences.

Jesus Christ is not the sole revelation of God; he is the sole Savior. The unique thing that happens in Christ is the act of reconciliation.

This is a unique event enacted in history, and something absolutely new in the world. The dramatic historical character of the Christ event tends to be diminished by the inflation of revelation as an answer to the modern question of how people attain knowledge of God. The assumption that the question of reconciliation and forgiveness is no longer the central human concern does not correspond either to the biblical message or the human condition as people experience it today.

The Authority of Scripture

The Christian doctrine of salvation in Christ alone is bound up with the authority of Scripture. Both affirmations stand and fall together. There are two dialectically related truths that form the necessary conditions for affirming the authority of the Bible. The first condition of biblical authority is that the Bible be used by the church to define its identity and mission, its being and doing, in the world. Where there is no church, there is no canon of Scripture and, of course, no need for it. The Bible will always be studied as sacred scripture only within the context of the church. Absent the fact of the church, the Bible is only an ancient collection of documents with no intrinsic authority for people today.

The Bible is acknowledged as authority only where the gospel of Jesus Christ is proclaimed within a worshiping community of believers. The Bible provides the point of reference by which the church understands its identity and mission in the world. Without the Bible the church is blind, and without the church the Bible is dumb. The church finds its identity in the Bible as the missionary people on the way to the nations with the gospel of Jesus Christ. The Bible is the norm for its ongoing faith and life. The church binds itself to the saving revelation of God in Jesus Christ according to the Scriptures and does not look for a new revelation above and beyond this one.

The second condition of biblical authority lies in its function as a medium of the authority of Jesus Christ himself. Christ is the Lord of Scripture. If we look at various accounts of biblical authority, they all witness to the promise, presence, and power of the gospel of Jesus Christ. What does the church know about God's self-revelation (Barth) apart from Christ? What is the meaning of salvation-history (Oscar Cullmann) without Christ as its midpoint? What is the content of the kerygma (Bultmann) apart from the Christ event? What is the meaning of the biblical symbols (Tillich) apart from their connection to the new being in Jesus as the Christ? How is the unifying end of universal history (Pannenberg) revealed apart from the proleptic event of Jesus' resurrection from the dead? For the Christian church and all individual believers, the ultimate authority of the Bible depends on its witness to Jesus Christ, who lived, died, and rose again for the world's salvation.

It is on account of Christ that the church confesses the authority of the Bible. The Scriptures are Christ centered. Luther's dictum, *"was Christum treibet,"* is still a useful way to speak of the Bible's authority, provided we do not apply it in a reductionistic manner.

By stressing these two conditions, the ecclesial context and the gospel content, we have unified what came apart in the conflict between Reformation and Roman Catholic theology. Roman Catholic doctrine has emphasized that the Bible is the book of the church, while, for Reformation theology, the Bible is the word of God. In the post-Reformation era, Protestant polemics tended to set Scripture against tradition. Now we know that this is not possible because the New Testament is a piece of the tradition of the early church.

Reformation doctrine emphasized that the living witness of the church points beyond its own tradition to what is ultimately the eschatological revelation of God in Jesus Christ. The teaching office of the church does not place itself above the authority of the living tradition of apostolic Christianity set forth in Scripture, but Scripture is not a norm outside the church. It functions as the norm; it conveys the word, communicates the Spirit, and awakens faith, only within the context of the preaching which founded and sustains the church.

A Chalcedonian Hermeneutic

Traditions that affirm the authority of Scripture may still disagree on what it says. The hermeneutical issue then becomes decisive. An ecumenically valid hermeneutic must be guided by the centrality of Christ in biblical revelation. The church's christological dogma is relevant to biblical interpretation. At the Council of Chalcedon (451 A.D.) there were two mutually opposed errors, the one stressing the human nature of Christ at the expense of the divine (Adoptianism), and the other stressing the divine nature at the expense of the human (Monophysitism). The truth is that the two natures with all their attributes are both completely present and, at the same time, inseparably united. By analogy the same applies to the Bible. The Bible is the word of God completely and irreducibly expressed in human words in all their time conditionedness.

We call this a Chalcedonian hermeneutic of biblical exegesis. At a Vatican gathering of biblical scholars in April 1993, Pope John Paul II delivered a remarkable address to celebrate the one hundredth anniversary of *Providentissimus Deus* and the fiftieth of *Divino afflante Spiritu*. He dealt with the importance of the historical-critical study of the Bible for the faith and life of the church. He warned against "the individualist illusion that one can better understand the texts outside the community of believers."[21] The texts do not exist, the Pope reminds biblical exegetes, to satisfy the curiosity of individual scholars or to provide them with subject matter to investigate on the basis of philosophical presuppositions opposed to the Christian truth.

The dominant thrust of the post-Enlightenment tradition of biblical criticism has been to emancipate itself from the church's faith and doctrine. Because there is no such thing as exegesis without presuppositions, critical exegesis will be conducted either on the basis of churchly or some other presuppositions. The Pope's address asserts harmony between Christian belief in the mystery of the incarnation and a full affirmation of the use of the historical-critical method: "The Church of Christ takes the realism of the incarnation seriously, and this is why she attaches great importance to the 'historico-critical' study of the Bible."[22]

Christian biblical scholars may and must use all the available methods, findings, and insights of critical biblical scholarship. Just as the Word became flesh—without one being changed into the other or separated from the other, as Chalcedon taught—so we have treasures of divine revelation in vessels of human language and history. Let the historical exegetes examine these vessels to their heart's content. "None of the human aspects of language can be neglected. . . . Studying the human circumstances of the Word of God should be pursued with ever renewed interest."[23]

Continuing with the Chalcedonian analogy, we must also assert that the historical critical approach is not enough. The Pope said:

> In order to respect the coherence of the church's faith and of scriptural interpretation, Catholic exegesis must be careful not to limit itself to the human aspects of the biblical texts. . . . Catholic exegesis does not focus its attention on only the human aspects of biblical revelation, which is sometimes the mistake of the historico-critical method, or on only the divine aspects, as fundamentalism would have it; it strives to highlight both of them as they are united in the divine "condescension," which is the basis of all Scripture.[24]

Historical criticism divorced from the church's faith and life serves a different master than the Word of God incarnate. It is simply not as objective, neutral, and free as often its practitioners imagine. If biblical scholars do not conduct their research within the framework of the Christian vision of ultimate reality and truth, they will necessarily proceed on some other premises, acknowledged or not. Often the premises are hidden or disguised, but "you will know them by their fruits (Matt. 7:16)." The Christian exegete will not embark on fanciful hypotheses out of harmony with the mystery of the incarnation.

The Pope has struck a chord common to all Christian scholars who share the same evangelical catholic faith and have also experienced the dead end of a critical methodology applied in separation from the church's belief in the mystery of the incarnation.

CHAPTER EIGHT

The Future of Lutheranism in America

THIS CHAPTER FOCUSES on the present agony and prospects for the future of Lutheranism in America from theological and ecclesiological perspectives. I make no pretense to be unbiased nor do I attempt to base my judgments and proposals on social-scientific grounds. All my reflections are filtered through the lens of my own participation in the theological struggles of our time to define the meaning of being Lutheran in America. We are engaged, I believe, in a fierce struggle for the soul of Lutheranism as a confessing movement in continuity with the original intention of the Reformation and as expressed in the Augsburg Confession. We are not contending against flesh and blood, but against powers and principalities in high places that are stronger and more numerous than we are.

James Davison Hunter has written the much publicized book *Culture Wars: The Struggle to Define America*.[1] It deals with the controversial issues of family, art, education, law, and politics. His analysis of the *Kulturkampf* now being waged between two parties that he calls "progressives" and "orthodox" is given from the perspective of what a sociologist can see, measure, and objectively describe. We, on the other hand, are dealing with a *Kirchenkampf* not nearly so objectifiable and subject to scientific controls. The battle is not merely between liberals and conservatives, progressives and orthodox, but between divine and antidivine forces that grapple anonymously behind the backs of our visible parties and party platforms. Within the church everyone claims that God is on their side. No one advances a proposal, no matter how novel or heretical, with a warning that God is on the other side. I do not see things objectively as a social scientist claims, nor do I see things transcendentally from God's point of view, as a prophet claims. I agree with the Chinese proverb that says, "To prophesy is very difficult, especially with respect to the future."

I would confess to be a partisan—one member of a struggle group committed to a cause with special interests—trying to win over the hearts and minds of people with a different and perhaps even an opposing set of interests. We are doing battle over an agenda that has to do with what we believe about the triune God, salvation through Christ alone; the sanctifying work of the Holy Spirit through the church; true preaching of the word and faithful administration of the Sacraments; the divine institution of the holy ministry signified by the sacramental character of ordination (*Apology*, Article XIII); the ecumenical work promoting the oneness of the church; and the great commission of our Lord to go with the gospel to the plurality of nations, to teach and to baptize that people from all other religions may come to believe in Christ and become members of his church. This is no small order, but nothing less will do. Many folks in the church are asleep while their church is being taken hostage by a belief system incompatible with the Christian faith. Many others do not like the struggle metaphor, preferring, instead, the policy of appeasement and accommodation for the sake of peace and harmony, as the necessary condition of institutional growth and financial success. We are merely asked to fight a good fight; we are not in the business of awarding prizes.

The Legacy of Protestant Liberalism

In an article published in *Pro Ecclesia,* Michael Hollerich wrote about an exchange of letters between Erik Peterson and Adolf von Harnack.[2] Peterson was a good Protestant who became disillusioned with liberal theology, began a friendship with Karl Barth, held a professorship on the Protestant faculty at Bonn University, and, when he became convinced of the illegitimacy of Lutheranism, he converted to the Roman Catholic Church.

Harnack conceded that the "formal principle" of traditional

Protestantism, that is, the *sola scriptura* principle, could no longer be maintained in a critically responsible way. A pure biblicism anchored in a strict doctrine of verbal inspiration would seem to provide Protestantism with a sure authority, but today, Harnack admitted, to believe that is both religiously and theologically naive. The moment one retreats from pure biblicism, one needs to supplement biblical authority with the authority of the apostolic tradition, which includes within itself the canonical authority of Holy Scripture as well as the dogmatic authority of the church expressed in its Creed and its Office. Peterson said, "Without any dogmatic authority there can be no church."[3] Then he said,

> The evangelical (Protestant) church couldn't take a position on relevant questions, because a "standpoint" was impossible given the lack of a dogmatic basis. All that remained was the non-binding character of a moral exhortation. . . . I see clearly that the evangelical church submits itself to every influence, but in the process gives itself away."[4]

These words were written in Germany in 1928, not in present-day America. That, Harnack conceded, was the inevitable nature of modern Protestantism, something he much applauded, in preference to the authoritarianism of previous Catholic and Reformation models of authority.

Harnack said, "Protestantism must confess frankly that it does not want to be and cannot be a church in the manner of the Catholic church, that it repudiates all formal authorities."[5] In fact, Harnack acknowledged that in Protestantism every theologian happily goes his own way. Is it not the same way today? There is no binding authority—not the authority of the church or the authority of the Bible. The only authority is that of the collective thoughts and experiences of the people, funneled into the pseudodemocratic egalitarian system, who who get together in synod assemblies every two years to vote their non-binding opinions on every subject under the sun.

Harnack wrote his seven volumes of the *History of Dogma* as a critical dissolution of dogma, terminating in the pure subjectivity of Luther's living faith. That, he noted, is the end of dogma, the end of ecclesial authority. After that, Harnack said, you have the continuation of the subjective-religious line of Anabaptism, Pietism, Enlightenment Lutheranism, and Schleiermacherism—in other words, modern Protestantism. "In the meantime," Harnack said, "we are still severely dependent on the remains of Catholic tradition among us, as it were, on the aroma of an empty bottle."[6] We have two alternatives, "either to lead Protestantism back to Catholicism (be it of the Greek or Roman variety), or to ground it in an absolute biblicism."[7] Harnack added, "both alternatives are closed off, closed off because they stand in contradiction to our historical knowledge."[8] In answer to the question, what will then become of the evangelical church, Harnack answers, "I do not know."[9]

Peterson, for a time, welcomed Barth's attempt to recover what Harnack called "the ancient Catholic element of traditional Protestantism."[10] After all, Barth wrote church dogmatics; he brought back the doctrine of the Trinity, the Logos Christology, and the theology of the church fathers and the ecumenical councils. Fine, but Barth's theology belongs to no particular church. In Protestantism, Peterson says, developments in church and theology proceed independently of each other. No church is obligated to take Barth seriously, and Barth, as a theologian, was not subject to the authority of any particular church. The result according to Peterson is "that the theologian shakes his head at 'the man of the church,' because he has no connection at all with theology, and 'the man of the church' at the theologian, who confronts the concrete tasks of the church so uncomprehendingly."[11]

This opposition between the theologian and the churchman was concretely played out in the 1930s in a controversial exchange between Barth and Bishop Otto Dibelius. This exchange underscored for Peterson the idea that in Protestantism it is possible for the church to exist without any serious relation to dogma and theology, and it is possible for theology to be carried on in the faculties as a kind of free-floating philosophy of religion without any attention to the concrete problems of church life. As Peterson said, "Protestant theology will always remain more or less the private concern of professors of theology; and thus nothing is actually affected by the greater or lesser degree of an individual's church affiliation."[12]

Such a state of affairs was not a mere peculiarity of church and theology in Germany in the 1930s. Think of the thousands of theological professors who scramble to get on the annual program to read papers at the American Academy of Religion and the Society of Biblical Literature, few of those papers have a scintilla of significance for what is going on in the life of the church. If Peterson could charge the German Protestant church and Protestant theology with a "dogmatic deficit" in his day, in agreement with Barth, how much more true is that of church and theology in Protestant America?

The premise underlying Peterson's diagnosis is that modern Protestantism is a far cry from traditional Reformation Protestantism. To be sure, traditional Protestantism had no dogma, in a strict sense, because it had no magisterium. It, however, "possessed a kind of quasi-dogma in its various confessional documents, which had a dignity analogous to that of dogma, to the degree that, and so long as, the state guarded the binding legitimacy of these confessions."[13] Once Protestantism becomes completely a conglomeration of voluntary associations—which it has become in modern times, especially in America—its historic confessional writings are remembered mainly as monuments of its classical heritage. When they are officially subscribed, they are not necessarily believed, and where they are believed, they have no binding character. Who would there be to insure that?

Peterson reminds us that traditional Protestantism derived and sustained its meaning, theologically and ecclesiologically, by its special relation to Catholicism. "Traditional Protestantism," he said, "had an awareness of a fundamental, dialectical kinship with the mother church; even in the worst exaggerations of confessional polemics, it remained bonded to the old church."[14] It lived off of the Catholic elements in its own reality. Its bishops stood in historical connection with the bishops of the Catholic age. Its liturgical worship remained close to the Roman mass. Its confessions reaffirmed the dogmatic truths of the ecumenical councils and claimed to be teaching nothing new. It emphatically rejected heresies old and new that kept intruding into the church. It even retained elements of medieval scholasticism, along with its methods and problems, linked with Aristotelian philosophy. Even Pietism presupposed the dogmatic foundations of orthodoxy, even while it recuperated elements of the spirituality of medieval mysticism.

Peterson correctly observed that the history of Protestantism has witnessed a progressive alienation from the Catholic elements written into its origins. He spoke of a "slippage in the foundations,"[15] and noted that "the ontological basis of Protestantism has changed."[16] When Protestantism embarked on its own prodigal self-authenticating journey independent of mother church, it has taken recourse to three alternatives, which are much in vogue in Protestantism today, to establish itself publicly as a legitimate church.

One alternative to a church based on pure doctrine is to translate theology into universal truths of reason that conform to and legitimate the contemporary *Zeitgeist*, to resymbolize the historic faith according to the prevailing assumptions of modernity. A second alternative is mysticism, but when Christian mysticism loses its dogmatic basis, it degenerates into mere feeling, into forms of spirituality spawned by secularized mysticism and nourished by revivals of paganism. A third alternative leads to social activism; that is, works of love in pursuit of justice will supposedly guarantee the truth for which the church stands. Peterson said, as though he possessed the gift of foreknowledge, "All three of them are still today zealously championed, but it needs no great perceptiveness to realize that none of them necessarily is conducive to the goal of evangelical church life and theology, and they may even stand in opposition to the Reformation's original impetus."[17]

The Protestantization of Lutheranism in America

Peterson was writing about Protestantism in Germany in the 1930s. I am concerned with Lutheranism in America in the 1990s and beyond. Perhaps we Lutherans think we have been spared the fate of modern Protestantism. That is what many of us believed and taught for decades until we awakened from our dogmatic slumbers. Some among us made a big point about Lutherans not getting melted down into a Protestant lump. We were encouraged, even by outsiders, to believe that somehow we were different from other Protestants.

In 1961 Winthrop Hudson ended his book *American Protestantism* on a note flattering to Lutherans. He wrote,

The final prospect for a vigorous renewal of Protestant life and witness rests with the Lutheran churches. . . . Among the assets immediately at hand among the Lutherans are a confessional tradition, a
surviving liturgical structure, and a sense of community.[18]

Thirty years later Mark Noll of Wheaton College reiterated Hudson's
point saying, "The starting point of Lutheran thought, to its credit, is,
in George Lindbeck's words, 'neither biblicistic nor experientialist, and
certainly not individualistic, but dogmatic.'"[19] What Lutheran theologians "share with their confidence in dogma could bring welcome
refreshment to the American church."[20]

Will anyone care to tell Hudson and Noll, two Protestants, that
the emperor has no clothes, that Lutherans are rapidly joining the
parade of Protestant pluralism? Can anyone seriously argue that
Lutherans have sufficiently retained the vitalities of those Catholic elements in their foundational charter to catalytically revitalize the declining mainline denominations in America? Haven't the confessional
dogmatics, the chief source of the great expectations of Hudson and
Noll, practically given way to the progressivist agendas of today—therapeutic religion, multiculturalist ideology, inclusivity quotas, new age
spirituality, entertainment evangelism, lowest common denominator
ecumenism, pantheistic ecomysticism, radical post- and anti-Christian
feminism, liberationist crusades of every ilk, and a plethora of other
politically correct concerns? Where would you look for the confessional
dogmatics that keeps itself in faithful continuity with the great tradition of Western Catholic and Eastern Orthodox Christianity? Would
you look at the seminaries? Would you look at what the bishops say in
their pastoral letters? Would you look in the catalog of church publishing houses? Would you look at the bulk of materials emanating out of
church headquarters? If you did look, would you find anything to dis-
tinguish Lutheranism substantially from other Protestant denominations that trace their lineage back to the Reformation period? What you
would find is much evidence that shows the progressive and cumulative
reduction of Lutheranism into modern liberal Protestantism.

Another way to put the matter is that Samuel Schmucker's
proposal for Americanizing Lutheranism, which was rebuffed by the

nineteenth-century confessional renewal movement, is winning out in the reorganized church of latter-day Lutherans. David Gustafson has written the history of the American Lutheran controversy in a new book entitled *Lutherans in Crisis: The Question of Identity in the American Republic*, and he ends his account by showing that "the uneasy balance between loyalty to the Lutheran Confessions and accommodation to American culture has appeared once again to shift toward accommodation."[21] He cites three factors: first, an overzealous ecumenism that rushes to full communion with Protestant churches without concern for the doctrinal issues that occasioned separation in the first place; second, an over-heated program of social activism that locates the gospel in deeds not creeds, that sneers at the call to biblical and confessional faithfulness as the last gasp of the old white male patriarchal and nostalgically Eurocentric power brokers; and third, Lutheran churches in America, not least those that claim to be more "confessional than thou," have opened wide the doors of hospitality to the alien ecclesiology of the church growth movement.

Each of these three factors is a response to Lutheran anxiety about not making it on American soil. At times Lutheran ecumenism seems to be born out of a kind of pragmatism that sees the old lines of conflict, marking distinctions between Lutheranism and other forms of Protestantism, as irrelevant. Its social activism is born out of a feeling of guilt for being charged with quietism on ethical frontiers, the allegedly paralyzing effect of the two kingdoms doctrine. Getting on the church growth bandwagon is a frantic reaction to prevailing fear of declining membership, even though it means jazzing up the liturgy to appeal to baby boom consumers of religion.

The three alternatives to the confessional dogmatics of traditional Lutheranism of which Peterson spoke (rationalism, mysticism, and activism) are not exactly the same three that Gustafson cites (pragmatic ecumenism, social activism, and church growth evangelism), but they are similar in that both sets represent the collapse of dogma and its binding authority in church and theology. The upshot is that the church loses its catholic substance. Protestantism tries to re-create the church from "the aroma of an empty bottle"; it becomes vulnerable to the culture wars and has no means of defending itself from the hostile forces of American neopagan religion.

Harold Bloom has some poignant things to say about this American neopagan religion that is becoming increasingly more dominant in the pulpits, pews, and bureaus of the Protestant denominations. American religion has provided a happy home for the alien god of Gnosticism, the hallmark of which is experiential faith divorced from dogma. Bloom writes, "the American Religion, for its two centuries of existence, seems to me irretrievably Gnostic."[22] If Gnosticism ever died, it has been born again in America, "an obsessed society wholly in the grip of a dominant Gnosticism."[23] According to Bloom, "Gnosticism . . . is now, and always has been, the hidden religion of the United States, the American Religion proper."[24] "The God of the American Religion is an experiential God, so radically within our own being as to become a virtual identity with what is most authentic (oldest and best) in the self."[25] "Ancient Gnosticism was an elite religion, or quasi-religion; the oddity of our American Gnosis is that it is a mass phenomenon. There are tens of millions of Americans whose obsessive idea of spiritual freedom violates the normative basis of historical Christianity, though they are incapable of realizing how little they share of what once was considered Christian doctrine."[26]

Thousands of these Gnostics are welcomed into our churches at the front door and become members without benefit of serious catechization. Gallup-style findings show that American believers are religious in a general sense with scarcely no correlation to the specific beliefs of historic Christianity. They become church members without becoming Christian, baptized without believing in the biblical sense. It is no wonder that every year as much human traffic goes out the back door as comes in through the front.

Sociologists Benton Johnson, Dean R. Hoge, and Donald A. Luidens have published their discovery that the real reason for the decline of the mainline churches is lack of belief, by which they mean "orthodox Christian belief, and especially the teaching that a person can be saved only through Jesus Christ."[27] What they found is that the majority of members are "lay liberals" who have no clear understanding of what Christianity is or why they are Christian. They vaguely know that Christianity has something to do with belief in God and respect for Jesus and the Golden Rule. Somehow, Johnson, Hoge, and Luidens say, the "churches lost the will or the ability to teach the Christian faith and what it requires to a succession of younger cohorts in such a way as to command their allegiance."[28] "Lay liberals do not care what theological views their children embrace or whether they attend church when they grow up, but they do want them to become 'good people.'"[29] "Most lay liberals 'prefer' Christianity to other faiths, but they are unable to ground their preference in strong truth claims. . . . Some believe that a common thread of truth runs through all the world's major religions and that at the base all religions teach the same thing."[30]

These lay liberals embody perfectly Bloom's thesis about the essence of Gnosticism. Johnson, Hoge, and Luidens lamentably end their article with no suggestion of the likelihood of a turnabout, but they lay down the gauntlet: "If the mainline churches want to regain their vitality, their first step must be to address theological issues head-on."[31]

Bloom quotes Dietrich Bonhoeffer's lament, "God has granted American Christianity no Reformation."[32] But Bloom prefers the Gnosticism we've got to a reaffirmation of the Reformation. He says, "A neo-orthodox revival of Continental Reformed [he means Reformation] Protestantism is precisely what we do not need."[33] Bonhoeffer put his finger on the difference, which is precisely the dogmatic deficit in the American Religion. Bonhoeffer wrote, after observing what Peterson predicted was bound to happen in Protestantism, "It has been given to Americans less than any other people in the world to achieve the visible unity of the church of God on earth. It has been given to Americans more than any other people in the world to manifest a pluralism of Christian beliefs and denominations."[34] Further, Bonhoeffer observed, "The rejection of Christology is characteristic of the whole of present-day American theology. Christianity basically amounts to religion and ethics in American theology. Consequently, the person and work of Christ fall into the background and remain basically not understood in this theology."[35]

As Peterson said, "There is no dogma in the strict sense in the Protestant church, and so no theology is possible either. For there is no theology without dogmatics and no dogmatics without dogma."[36] In a letter to Harnack, Peterson wrote, "But can we count on interest in the history of dogma, once dogma has been expunged, once the 'formal authority' of dogma has been discarded in the church? What kind of interest can one still have in the history of the church, when there is no longer a church?"[37] Without the undergirding of dogma and the authority to mediate its truth-claims as the paradigmatic horizon within which the church is to believe, teach, and confess Jesus Christ to the world today, the church becomes fractionized into a multiplicity of sects "tossed to and fro and carried about with every wind of doctrine, by the cunning of men, by their craftiness in deceitful wiles (Eph. 4:14)." Peterson complained to Harnack in 1928, "I see the mentality of American denominations and American seminaries emerging in our student body. I see clearly how the church becomes a sect. . . . The standards in the church are sinking."[38]

A Proposal for the Future

We are at a crossroads in American Lutheranism. Willy-nilly we must choose which road to take. We may choose the road that continues in the line of Americanizing Lutheranism, making it one among many Protestant denominations that reflect all the deficits Peterson enumerated. We may individually take the road that leads back to Rome or East to Orthodoxy, as a few intelligent and sensitive Lutheran pastors have done. We may join one of the groups that seek to recover a kind of confessional Lutheranism we have known in the past, and there are still a few left who will pitch their battle in defense of the literal inerrancy of the Bible.

Another option I propose, only as an immediate interim strategy, is to look for paths of renewal that move through and across the denominations, working for a common future in which Christians and churches will visibly confess the one apostolic faith in one eucharistic fellowship. Lutherans will be wise to look for allies wherever we can find them and not go fishing only in Lutheran fjords. This is an ecumenical road and, as such, not a new one, but one whose plausibility and relevance are seriously being questioned by those taking other roads. Whether one is Lutheran, Episcopalian, Presbyterian, Methodist, or something else does not matter much in terms of the current struggles for the basic biblical contents of faith, the authority of dogma and confession, and fidelity to the gospel in eucharistic fellowship. While the ecclesial substance of the Protestant denominations is dissolving into the poisoned gruel of the American religion, whether on the fundamentalist right or the progressivist left, there are struggle groups within each dedicated to the renewal of the evangelical and catholic elements inherent in the originating impulses of the various Protestant traditions. There may have been some wild reformers who intended to start a Bible church without catholic substance, but Luther, Calvin, and Wesley were not among them. Nevertheless, in all the churches that bear their stamp, there has been a diminishment of catholic substance and orthodox doctrine coupled with a syncretic amalgamation of neopagan elements.

The strategy of the confessional Lutherans, or, as some call them, radical Lutherans, aims to strengthen Lutheran identity but requires as its essential precondition the continuation of the old anticatholic polemics, only now in more polite terms. It's as though they wished, for the sake of keeping the consciousness of Lutheran identity intact, that Vatican II had never happened, and that the national and international Catholic-Lutheran dialogues had not achieved convergence and consensus on church-dividing issues, as though it were better to have lived in a preecumenical age. Some confessional Lutherans oppose the proposal to remove the sixteenth-century anathemas that Lutherans and Roman Catholics formulated to condemn each other. Certain confessional Lutherans still invest their identity in an anti-Catholicism that is anachronistic in an ecumenical age.

Those of us who founded the Center for Catholic and Evangelical Theology are not willing to settle for becoming merely a miniconfessing movement within a Lutheranism sliding into mainstream Protestantism in America. We are committed to a broader realignment of those minds and hearts that stand, across denominational borders, on the common ground of the catholic and evangelical substance of the faith. This is an ecumenism inspired by the vision of full communion among catholic, orthodox, and evangelical communities in the East and West. Meanwhile, as confessional Lutherans feeling somewhat homeless in a culture-conforming denomination, we may contribute what we can to the actualization of this wider ecumenical vision by strengthening the catholic elements that still survive in our own Reformation tradition.[39] We can do this as a network of faithful pastors, bishops, and laity who will not surrender the church to the spirit of the age.

Lutheranism, by its very nature, is a part of the Western Catholic stream of Christianity. It shares the same belief in the triune God; in Jesus Christ as Lord and Savior; and in the Holy Spirit who calls, gathers, enlightens, and sanctifies the whole Christian church on earth. It confesses its faith in the one, holy, catholic, and apostolic church which gathered and transmitted to later generations the canonical writings of the Old and New Testaments as the authoritative document of God's revealing and reconciling activity for the salvation of the world. Lutherans and Western Catholics share the same ecumenical creeds and sacred liturgies; the same sacraments of baptism and holy communion; the same dominically instituted office of the holy ministry; and the same genealogies of apostles, martyrs, missionaries, saints, hymn writers, and doctors of the church. It would be committing spiritual suicide to embark on an ecumenical future with liberal Protestants of perpetual and widening separation from the Roman Catholic Church. One of the hallmarks of the American neopagan religion, with its Gnosticism and antinomianism, is precisely its rejection of all external authority. Tom Wolfe writes in his essay, "The Me Decade and the Third Great Awakening," that at the heart of the new religious consciousness lies "an axiom first propounded by the Gnostic Christians some eighteen hundred years ago: namely, that at the apex of every human soul there exists a spark of the light of God."[40] The church's claim to divine authority of its canon, creeds, eucharistic liturgy, and ordained ministry, is an offense to the gnostic mind-set because such external things inhibit the free expression of the divine flame enlightening each individual soul. The gnostic spirit manifests itself in anticlericalism, the rejection of ordination as a churchly act through which God sets aside persons today in apostolic succession both commissioning and empowering them to teach with authority. We are in the midst of an authority crisis that touches every aspect of the church's faith and life.

Protestant Gnostics, in the name of attacking the demons of

hierarchy, have broken down the supposedly heteronomous idols of ecclesial authority, but they are left with only the light of their inner sparks to put in the place of authority. The authority of ordained pastors in local congregations is still somewhat effective, but in other expressions of the church, including the churchwide assembly, the anticlerical and antihierarchical attitudes are pronounced. There is a magisterial vacuum which is being filled by the work of commissions and task forces selected on the basis of quotas.

What are the chances of a counteroffensive? Alisdair MacIntyre prophecies the coming of "new dark ages." He writes, "The barbarians are not waiting beyond the frontiers; they have been governing us for quite some time. And it is our lack of consciousness of this that constitutes part of our predicament."[41] If this is at all true about our culture, it applies in some measure to our culture-conforming churches. Where are the resources to respond to the challenges of our neopagan gnostic culture? Where does the buck stop? The future is not very promising unless there are ways to put a counteroffensive into active operation to bring some fresh vitamins into the anemic bodies of our mainline churches. Christians are not permitted to be fatalistic, to be as those who live with no hope in God. The possibility of a renewal of the confessing church option in our neopagan culture may not be precluded. Even in a pragmatic culture that prides itself in its science and technology, Christians are free to believe in miracles.

Whenever the established channels and structures of the organized churches are constipated with the ideological -isms of the age, church history teaches us that renewal movements arise spontaneously, first as protest and then as reconstruction. We are perhaps at a time when renewal will be spurred by a variety of voluntary struggle groups, institutes, centers, associations, and perhaps even new seminaries, that will spring up here and there, to promote faithfulness throughout the church to the word of God and to mine the ore of the great catholic and orthodox traditions, retrieving neglected treasures of the historic church—dogmatic, institutional, liturgical, and sapiential.

The recovery of authority in the church on matters of faith and morals cannot happen as long as the cord remains severed between ordination and magisterium. When the highest teaching authority is

this seems to be the very thing he deplores about Protestantism!

[handwritten margin notes: "for a college of bishops better able to know the mind of God?"]

the churchwide assembly composed of a minority of persons properly ordained to "judge doctrine and condemn doctrine that is contrary to the Gospel" (Augsburg Confession, Article XXVIII), the locus of authority in the church, which is signified by ordination, has been nullified and replaced by a system in which the laity are given the majority vote. Here there is a great confusion between spiritual authority and temporal power. Spiritual authority in the church should be exercised by those whom God has authorized "to preach the Gospel, to remit and retain sins, and to administer the sacraments" (Article XXVIII). Temporal power is something else. Here there is no problem if the laity are in the clear majority, voicing opinions and voting on worldly matters, because the church is not only a divine institution but also a human organization and, as such, subject to rules and regulations pertaining to the kingdom of God's left hand. What we have now is a massive confusion of authority and power in the church. The net result is a loss of sacred authority because the laity cannot be expected to teach with authority when they have not received, by ordination, the charism from the Holy Spirit to be teachers of the church and have not been empowered by theological education and pastoral experience to assume this solemn responsibility.

Another matter of high priority must be the recovery of the authority of Scripture. The teaching of the Bible in theological schools is in the grip of Gnosticism—the belief that it is necessary to appeal away from the plain sense of Scripture to a higher knowledge that lies above or behind the text. The aim of biblical studies is to put students in the know, so that they will be privy to an esoteric knowledge that even most intelligent and educated folks cannot get from their reading of the Scriptures in Hebrew, Greek, or English. The effect is paralysis on those not privy to this higher knowledge. The newly initiated are in bondage to their masters and cite their authority. Often their opinions stand in stark opposition to the biblical foundations of the classical dogmatics of the church, whether in their witness to the triune God, the divine-human person of Jesus Christ, and so forth. The result is an "ugly broad ditch"[42] between dogmatics that teaches what the church believes *(lex orandi lex credendi)* and exegesis that is obedient to the "papacy of sophisticated scholarship."[43] A deep hiatus runs through every seminary curriculum, as every somewhat alert student will quickly discover. The authority of the Bible is not autonomous. When people cease to believe in the church, they will soon cease to believe in the Bible. I can hardly imagine that the huge hiatus between exegesis and dogmatics will scarcely give way to a greater unity of theology until the divided churches resolve their differences into a greater unity of the church. For the Bible by itself, as Ernst Käsemann said, can be invoked to support a multiplicity of confessions.[44] If the Bible as a whole and in all its parts is not also read in light of the Holy Spirit at work in the early catholic church and later, the Bible will have no more authority than any other primitive document from antiquity.

I end without offering any pat formula for getting across the "ugly broad ditch." We must first realize that we are in the ditch. Peterson pointed to the ditch—the crisis of dogma and authority in the church in an age of historical relativism. The modern church cannot now claim to be in a much better position than G. E. Lessing when he cried, "That, then is the ugly, broad ditch which I cannot get across, however often and however earnestly I have tried to make the leap. If anyone can help me over it, let him do it, I beg him, I adjure him. He will deserve a divine reward from me."[45]

Notes

Notes to Introduction

1. Quoted by Joseph Ratzinger, "The Ecclesiology of the Second Vatican Council," *Communio* 11 (fall 1986): 239.

2. Ibid.

3. Numerous citations are provided by Henri de Lubac in *The Motherhood of the Church* (San Francisco: Ignatius Press, 1975), 47ff. See also Joseph C. Plumpe, *Mater Ecclesia* (Washington, D.C.: Catholic University of America Press, 1943).

4. Martin Luther, Large Catechism, in *The Book of Concord*, ed. and trans. Theodore G. Tappert (Philadelphia: Fortress Press, 1959), 416.

5. John Calvin, Book 4, Chapter 1, *Institutes of the Christian Religion*, trans. John Allen (Philadelphia: Presbyterian Board of Christian Education, 1813), 273–74.

6. Quoted by Henri de Lubac, *Christian Faith: The Structure of the Apostles' Creed* (London: Geoffrey Chapman, 1986), 104.

7. Ibid.

8. Friedrich Schleiermacher, *The Christian Faith*, ed. H. R. Mackintosh and J. S. Stewart (Edinburgh: T. & T. Clark, 1928), 103.

9. George Lindbeck, "A Protestant View of the Ecclesiological Status of the Roman Catholic Church," *Journal of Ecumenical Studies* 1/2 (1964): 244.

10. Paul McPartlan, *The Eucharist Makes the Church: Henri de Lubac and John Zizioulas in Dialogue* (Edinburgh: T. & T. Clark, 1993).

11. John Zizioulas, *Being as Communion* (Crestwood, N.Y.: St. Vladimir's Seminary Press, 1985), 15.

12. J.-M. R. Tillard, *Church of Churches: The Ecclesiology of Communion*, trans. R. C. De Peaux (Collegeville, Minn.: The Liturgical Press, 1992).

Notes to Chapter One

1. My use of this parable is indebted to George Lindbeck's article, "A Protestant View of the Ecclesiological Status of the Roman Catholic Church," *Journal of Ecumenical Studies* 1/2 (1964): 243–70.

2. Jaroslav Pelikan, *The Riddle of Roman Catholicism* (Nashville, Tenn.: Abingdon Press, 1959), 46.

3. Hans Küng, *The Council: Reform and Reunion*, trans. Cecily Hastings (New York: Sheed and Ward, 1961), 73.

4. Pelikan, *The Riddle of Roman Catholicism*, 196.

5. K. E. Skydsgaard, *One in Christ*, trans. Axel C. Kildegaard (Philadelphia: Muhlenberg Press, 1957), 37–38.

6. Lindbeck, "A Protestant View of the Ecclesiological Status of the Roman Catholic Church," *Journal of Ecumenical Studies*, 245.

7. Küng, *Reform and Reunion*, 76.

8. Skydsgaard, *One in Christ*, 43.

9. Hans Küng, *Justification: The Doctrine of Karl Barth and a Catholic Reflection* (New York: Thomas Nelson & Sons, 1964).

Notes to Chapter Two

1. "Protestant Hara-Kiri," *The Christian Century*, June 22, 1966; "Response, Demur," *The Christian Century*, August 17, 1966 (an exchange of views between the editor of the *Century* and myself); "The Braaten Brouhaha," *The Christian Century*, October 26, 1966. These editorial views were evoked by an article, which I had published in *Una Sancta*, entitled "Rome, Reformation, and Reunion," June 1966. The *Una Sancta* article was a shortened version of an address which I had printed in *The Record* of the Lutheran School of Theology, August 1965, under the title "The Tragedy of the Reformation and the Return to Catholicity." In the September, 1966, issue of *Una Sancta*, a symposium of responses to my article and *The Christian Century* editorial opinions was featured. Professors Albert Outler, Robert McAfee Brown, George Lindbeck, and Warren Quanbeck made contributions, on the whole favorable to the viewpoints which my article intended to set forth, in the symposium.

2. The idea for this image of Protestants in exile came from an article by George Lindbeck, "A Protestant View of the Ecclesiological Status of the Roman Catholic Church," *Journal of Ecumenical Studies*, 1/2 (1964): 243–70.

3. The editor compared Protestants to "Englishmen who left their

native land in protest and found on this continent their true and happy homeland and called it New England. Was it tragic that they did not return?"

4. Cf. Gustave Weigel, "Catholic Ecclesiology in Our Time," in *Christianity Divided*, ed. Daniel Callahan et al. (New York: Sheed & Ward, 1961), 177f.

5. Ibid., 179.

6. Ibid., 179–80.

7. Ibid., 177.

8. Cf. Yves Congar, "The Church: The People of God," *The Church and Mankind*, in *Concilium*, vol. 1 (New York: Paulist Press, 1965), 14–18.

9. Johannes B. Metz, a Roman Catholic theologian, is developing an understanding of the church along the lines of Pannenberg and Moltmann. See his essay, "The Church and the World," in *The Word in History*, ed. T. Patrick Burke (New York: Sheed & Ward, 1966). Some of my ideas in this essay bear an indebtedness to lectures by Pannenberg on the kingdom of God which he delivered at the Lutheran School of Theology at Chicago in January 1967.

10. The phrase is Pannenberg's. See n. 9.

11. The severest criticism of church-centered thinking is J. C. Hoekendijk's *The Church Inside Out* (Philadelphia: Westminster Press, 1964).

12. Rudolf Schnackenberg, *The Church in the New Testament* (New York: Herder & Herder, 1965), 26–27.

13. Ernst Käsemann, "Paulus und der Frühkatholizismus," *Exegetische Versuche und Besinnungen*, vol. 2 (Göttingen: Vandenhoek und Ruprecht, 1964), 239–52.

14. Leslie Dewart, *The Future of Belief* (New York: Herder & Herder, 1966), 127–28.

15. Dietrich Bonhoeffer, *Letters and Papers from Prison* (New York: Macmillan, 1971).

16. Paul Tillich, *Systematic Theology*, vol. 3 (Chicago: University of Chicago Press, 1963), 376.

Notes to Chapter Three

1. Quoted from Willi Marxsen, *Mark the Evangelist* (Nashville: Abingdon Press, 1969), 145.

2. Teilhard de Chardin, *The Future of Man* (London: Collins, 1964), 115.

3. H. Richard Niebuhr, *The Kingdom of God in America* (New York: Harper & Brothers, 1937).

4. See my chapter, "American Historical Experience and Christian Reflection," in *Projections: Shaping an American Theology for the Future* (Garden City, N.Y.: Doubleday, 1970).

5. Attributed to Gerhard Gloege, quoted by Wolfhart Pannenberg, in *Theology and the Kingdom of God* (Philadelphia: Westminster Press, 1969), 51.

6. Ibid.

7. Karl Barth, *The Epistle to the Romans* (London: Oxford University Press, 1933), 314.

8. For example, "Verheissung, Zeit-Erfüllung, Biblische Betrachtung," in *Zwischen den Zeiten*, 1931, 459.

9. Ibid., 459.

10. Tjarko Stadtland, *Eschatologie und Geschichte in der Theologie des jungen Karl Barth* (Neukirchen: Neukirchener Verlag, 1966), 189.

11. Martin Heidegger, *Being and Time* (London: SCM Press, 1962), 378.

12. Rudolf Bultmann, *Jesus and the Word* (New York: Charles Scribner's Sons, 1934), 51.

13. Ibid., 131.

14. Paul Tillich, "Historical and Nonhistorical Interpretations of History," in *The Protestant Era* (Chicago: University of Chicago Press, 1948), 20.

15. Paul Tillich, *Biblical Religion and the Search for Ultimate Reality* (Chicago: University of Chicago Press, 1955), 41.

16. Paul Tillich, *Systematic Theology*, vol. 3 (Chicago: University of Chicago Press, 1963), 400ff.

17. Pannenberg, *Theology and the Kingdom*, 53.

18. Jürgen Moltmann, *Religion, Revolution and the Future* (New York: Charles Scribner's Sons, 1969), 117ff.

19. *The Documents of Vatican II*, ed. Walter M. Abbott; trans. Joseph Gallagher (New York: Guild Press, 1966), 17.

20. Ibid., 17, n. 11.

21. "The church is the congregation of saints, in which the gospel is rightly taught and the sacraments are rightly administered."

22. See my chapter, "The Episcopate and the Petrine Offices as Expressions of Unity," in *Spirit, Faith, and Church*, by Wolfhart Pannenberg, Avery Dulles, Carl E. Braaten (Philadelphia: Westminster Press, 1970), 89ff.

23. J. C. Hoekendijk, *The Church Inside Out* (Philadelphia: Westminster Press, 1966), 71.

24. See Rosemary Radford Ruether, *The Radical Kingdom* (New York: Harper & Row, 1970), which deals in detail with the apocalyptic revolutionary movements in Western experience.

Notes to Chapter Four

1. G. E. Lessing, "On the Proof of the Spirit and of Power," in *Lessing's Theological Writings*, ed. H. Chadwick (London, 1956), 55.

2. Ibid.

3. Thomas Kuhn, *The Structure of Scientific Revolutions* (Chicago: University of Chicago Press, 1970).

4. *The Book of Concord: The Confessions of the Evangelical Lutheran Church*, trans. and ed. Theodore G. Tappert et al. (Philadelphia: Fortress Press, 1959), 465.

5. Martin Luther, Large Catechism, in *The Book of Concord*, ed. and trans. Theodore G. Tappert (Philadelphia: Fortress Press, 1959), 415–16.

6. Cyprian quoted by Walter Kasper, *The God of Jesus Christ*, trans. Matthew J. O'Connell (New York: Crossroad, 1984), 247.

7. See the proposals of J.-M. R. Tillard, *Church of Churches: The Ecclesiology of Communion*, trans. R. C. dePeaux (Collegeville, Minn.: The Liturgical Press, 1992).

8. Ernst Käsemann, "The Canon of the New Testament and the Unity of the Church," in *Essays on New Testament Themes*, trans. W. J. Montague (London: SCM Press, 1964), 103.

Notes to Chapter Five

1. Georges Florovsky, "Le corps du Christ vivant: Une interpretation orthodoxe de l'Église," *La Sainte Église Universelle* (Paris: Delachaux et Niestlé, 1948), 9.

2. See Paul Minear, *Images of the Church in the New Testament* (Philadelphia: Westminster Press, 1960); Avery Dulles, *Models of the Church* (Garden City, N.Y.: Doubleday & Co., 1974).

3. Conrad Bergendoff, *The Doctrine of the Church in American Lutheranism* (Philadelphia: Muhlenberg Press, 1956), 19.

4. Kent Knutson, *The Community of Faith and the Word: An Inquiry into the Concept of the Church in Contemporary Lutheranism* (Ann Arbor, Mich.: University Microfilms, Ind., 1961), 3.

5. N. P. Williams and Charles Harris, ed., *Northern Catholicism:*

Centenary Studies in the Oxford and Parallel Movements (London: SPCK, 1933), 478.

6. Ibid.

7. *The Book of Concord: The Confessions of the Evangelical Lutheran Church,* trans. and ed. Theodore G. Tappert et al. (Philadelphia: Fortress Press, 1959).

8. Ibid., 174–75.

9. Thomas C. Oden, "Confessions of a Grieving Seminary Professor," *Good News* (January/February 1994).

10. Walter Bauer, *Orthodoxy and Heresy in Earliest Christianity* (Philadelphia: Fortress Press, 1971).

11. Helmut Koester, "Epilogue: Current Issues in New Testament Scholarship," in *The Future of Early Christianity: Essays in Honor of Helmut Koester,* ed. Birger A. Pearson (Minneapolis: Fortress Press, 1991), 472.

12. I owe the skeleton of this typology to Ola Tjörhom, "'Heresy' and 'Unity in Faith'—The Problem of Heresy in Ecumenical Perspective," *Norsk Teologisk Tidsskrift* 4 (1993).

13. Heinrich Schmid, *The Doctrinal Theology of the Evangelical Lutheran Church,* trans. Charles A. Hay and Henry E. Jacobs (Minneapolis: Augsburg Publishing House, 1961), 100.

14. Dietrich Bonhoeffer, *Gesammelte Schriften,* vol. 3 (Munich: Kaiser Verlag, 1966), 206.

15. Ibid.

16. Article XIV, "Ecclesiastical Order," *Apology of the Augsburg Confession,* in *The Book of Concord,* 215.

Notes to Chapter Six

1. Albert Schweitzer, *The Quest of the Historical Jesus,* trans. W. Montgomery, 3rd ed. (London: Adam & Charles Black, 1954).

2. Paul Tillich, *Systematic Theology,* vol. 2 (Chicago: University of Chicago Press, 1957), 102.

3. Rudolf Bultmann, *Jesus and the Word,* trans. Louise Smith and Erminie Lantero (New York: Charles Scribner's Sons, 1934), 9.

4. Emil Brunner, *The Mediator,* trans. Olive Wyon (Philadelphia: Westminster Press, 1947), 187.

5. Ernst Käsemann, "The Problem of the Historical Jesus," in *Essays on New Testament Themes: Studies in Biblical Theology,* trans. W. J. Montague, no. 41 (Naperville, Ill.: Alec R. Allenson, 1964), 46.

6. Martin Kähler, *Der sogenannte historische Jesus und der*

geschichtliche, biblische Christus (Leipzig: A. Deichert, 1896). The book was reissued in 1956 by Christian Kaiser Verlag, Munich. The English translation appeared in 1964 (reissued 1988) by Fortress Press, translated, edited, and with an introduction by Carl E. Braaten. I tried to capture the flavor of Kähler's distinction between "*historisch*" and "*geschichtlich*" by the English words "historical" and "historic" respectively.

7. Francis Schüssler Fiorenza, *Foundational Theology: Jesus and the Church* (New York: Crossroad, 1984), 5.

8. N. T. Wright, *Who Was Jesus?* (Grand Rapids, Mich.: Wm. B. Eerdmans Publishing Company, 1993), 12.

9. Jaroslav Pelikan, *Jesus Through the Centuries* (New Haven: Yale University Press, 1985).

10. Schweitzer, *Historical Jesus*, 4.

11. *RGG*, 3rd ed. (1959), ET, *Jesus* (Philadelphia: Fortress Press, 1973), 5.

12. Schweitzer, *Historical Jesus*, 3.

13. S. G. F. Brandon, *Jesus and the Zealots: A Study of the Political Factor in Primitive Christianity* (Manchester: The University Press, 1967); Hugh J. Schonfield, *The Passover Plot* (London: Hutchison & Co. Ltd., 1965); Morton Smith, *The Secret Gospel: The Discovery and Interpretation of the Secret Gospel according to Mark* (New York: Harper, 1973); C. F. Potter, *The Last Years of Jesus* (New York: Fawcett Publications, 1958); Geza Vermes, *Jesus the Jew: A Historian's Reading of the Gospels* (New York: The Macmillan Company, 1973); Burton H. Mack, *A Myth of Innocence: Mark and Christian Origins* (Philadelphia: Fortress Press, 1988); John Dominic Crossan, *The Historical Jesus: The Life of a Mediterranean Jewish Peasant* (San Francisco: Harper & Row, 1991); Marcus Borg, *Jesus: A New Vision* (San Francisco: Harper & Row, 1987); Elisabeth Schüssler Fiorenza, *In Memory of Her: A Feminist Theological Reconstruction of Christian Origins* (New York: Crossroad, 1983); Barbara Thiering, *Jesus the Man: A New Interpretation from the Dead Sea Scrolls* (Sydney, Australia: Doubleday, 1992); A. N. Wilson, *Jesus* (London: Sinclair-Stevenson, 1992); and John Spong, *Born of a Woman: A Bishop Rethinks the Birth of Jesus* (San Francisco: Harper & Row, 1992).

14. Pelikan, *Jesus Through Centuries*, 220.

15. *The Christian Century*, July 28–August 4, 1993.

16. Brevard S. Childs, *Biblical Theology of the Old and New Testaments: Theological Reflection on the Christian Bible* (Minneapolis: Fortress Press, 1993).

17. Jon D. Levinson, *The Hebrew Bible, The Old Testament and*

Historical Criticism: Jews and Christians in Biblical Studies (Philadelphia: Westminster/John Knox Press, 1993).

18. *The Christian Century,* July 28–August 4, 1993, 743.

19. Ibid., 744.

20. Ibid., 746.

21. Ibid., 747.

22. Ibid.

23. October 13, 1993, 994-997.

24. Ibid., 995.

25. Jon D. Levinson, "The Bible: Unexamined Commitments of Criticism," *First Things,* no. 30 (February, 1993). This article appeared in a somewhat different version in his book *The Hebrew Bible, the Old Testament, and Historical Criticism: Jews and Christians in Biblical Studies.*

26. Levinson, "The Bible," *First Things,* 30.

27. Ibid., 31.

28. Ibid., 32.

29. Ibid., 32.

30. Wright, *Who Was Jesus?,* ix.

31. Ibid., 18.

32. Ibid., 81.

33. Ibid., 59.

34. Ibid., 95.

35. Ibid., 96.

36. *Time,* May 7, 1979.

37. Cf. Geza Vermes, *Jesus the Jew,* and, twenty years later, *The Religion of Jesus the Jew* (Minneapolis: Fortress, 1993).

38. Vermes, *The Religion of Jesus the Jew,* 210.

39. Ibid., 210–12.

40. Ibid., 213.

41. Cf. Walter Kasper and Gerhard Sauter, "The Church as Sacrament of the Spirit," in *Kirche—Ort des Geistes* (Freiburg: Herder, 1976), 12–55.

42. The English text is available in *Origins,* CNS Documentary Service, vol. 23, no. 29 (January 6, 1994), 497–524.

43. Ibid., 515.

Notes to Chapter Seven

1. Paul Tillich, *Systematic Theology,* vol. 1 (Chicago: University of Chicago Press, 1951), 3.

2. Ibid., 40, 42.

3. Ibid., 45.

4. Ibid., 46.

5. Ibid., 50.

6. Ibid., 43.

7. George A. Lindbeck, *The Nature of Doctrine: Religion and Theology in a Postliberal Age* (Philadelphia: Westminster Press, 1984).

8. Eberhard Jüngel, *God as the Mystery of the World*, trans. Darrell L. Guder (Grand Rapids, Mich.: Eerdmans, 1983), viii.

9. Paul Tillich, "The Two Types of Philosophy of Religion," in *Theology of Culture* (New York: Oxford University Press, 1959).

10. Paul Tillich, *A History of Christian Thought* (New York: Harper & Row, 1968), 186.

11. Karl Barth, *Letters, 1961–1968,* trans. and ed. Geoffrey W. Bromiley (Grand Rapids, Mich.: Eerdmans, 1981), 179.

12. Ibid., 228.

13. Ibid., 182.

14. John Macquarrie, *Principles of Christian Theology* (New York: Charles Scribner's Sons, 1966), 48–52.

15. Peter Berger, *A Rumor of Angels* (Garden City, N.Y.: Doubleday, 1969), 90.

16. Paul Tillich, *Systematic Theology,* vol. 2 (Chicago: University of Chicago Press, 1957), 27.

17. Langdon Gilkey, *Naming the Whirlwind: The Renewal of God Language* (Indianapolis: Bobbs-Merrill Co., 1969), 20.

18. Sharon D. Welch, *Communities of Resistance and Solidarity: A Feminist Theology of Liberation* (Maryknoll, N.Y.: Orbis Books, 1985), 1.

19. Ibid., 2.

20. Paul Althaus, "Die Inflation des Begriffs der Offenbarung in der gegenwärtigen Theologie," *Zeitschrift für systematische Theologie* 18 (1941): 134–49.

21. *L'Osservatore Romano*, n. 17 (1288), April 28, 1993, 6.

22. Ibid.

23. Ibid.

24. Ibid.

Notes to Chapter Eight

1. James Davison Hunter, *Culture Wars: The Struggle to Define America* (San Francisco: HarperCollins Publishers, 1991).

2. Michael Hollerich, "Erik Peterson's Correspondence with Adolf von Harnack: Retrieving a Neglected Critique of Church, Theology, and Secularization in Weimar Germany," in *Pro Ecclesia, A Journal of Catholic and Evangelical Theology* 2/3 (1993), 305–32.

3. "Correspondence with Harnack and an Epilogue," *Pro Ecclesia,* 334.

4. Ibid., 334.

5. Ibid., 335.

6. Ibid., 338.

7. Ibid., 337.

8. Ibid., 337.

9. Ibid., 338.

10. Ibid., 338.

11. Ibid., 339.

12. Ibid., 340.

13. Ibid., 341.

14. Ibid., 341–42.

15. Ibid., 342.

16. Ibid., 342.

17. Ibid., 343.

18. Winthrop S. Hudson, *American Protestantism* (Chicago: University of Chicago Press, 1961), 176.

19. Mark Noll, "Ethnic, American, or Lutheran? Dilemmas for a Historic Confession in the New World," *Lutheran Theological Seminary Bulletin*, Gettysburg, 71:1 (Winter, 1991), 31.

20. Ibid.

21. David A. Gustafson, *Lutherans in Crisis* (Minneapolis: Fortress Press, 1993), 49.

22. Harold Bloom, *The American Religion* (New York: Simon & Schuster, 1992), 49.

23. Ibid.

24. Ibid., 50.

25. Ibid., 259.

26. Ibid., 263.

27. Benton Johnson, Dean R. Hoge, and Donald A. Luidens, "Mainline Churches: The Real Reason for Decline," *First Things* 31 (March 1993), 15.

28. Ibid., 18.

29. Ibid., 16.

30. Ibid., 15.

31. Ibid., 18.

32. Bloom, *American Religion*, 259.

33. Ibid.

34. Dietrich Bonhoeffer, "Protestantismus ohne Reformation," *Gesammelte Schriften*, ed. Eberhard Bethge (Munich: Chr. Kaiser Verlag, 1958), 325.

35. Ibid., 352.

36. Hollerich, "Erik Peterson's Correspondence," 340.

37. Ibid., 337.

38. Ibid.

39. In October 1994, the Center for Catholic and Evangelical Theology sponsored conferences, "The Catholicity of the Reformation," both in Northfield, Minn., and Lancaster, Pa., to examine the viability of this proposal.

40. Philip Lee, *Against the Protestant Gnostics* (London/New York: Oxford University Press, 1987), 197.

41. Quoted in Hunter, *Culture Wars*, 315.

42. G. E. Lessing, "On the Proof of the Spirit and of Power," in *Lessing's Theological Writings*, ed. H. Chadwick (London, 1956), 55.

43. Martin Kähler, *The So-called Historical Jesus and the Historic Biblical Christ*, trans. Carl E. Braaten (Philadelphia: Fortress Press, 1988).

44. Ernst Käsemann, "The Canon of the New Testament and the Unity of the Church," in *Essays on New Testament Themes*, trans. W. J. Montague (London: SCM Press, 1964), 95–107.

45. Lessing, "On the Proof of the Spirit and of Power," 55.

Index of Persons and Subjects